THE
CHURCH
AND THE
BODY
POLITIC

THE CHURCH AND THE BODY POLITIC

Franklin H. Littell

THE SEABURY PRESS
New York

Copyright © 1969 by The Seabury Press, Incorporated
Library of Congress Catalog Card Number: 68–29988
Design by Nancy H. Dale
622-1168-C-35
Printed in the United States of America

▶ PREFACE

FOR some time, a chief obstacle in the way of effective witness by the American churches has been a self-identity problem.

Some spokesmen for the churches, and not all from the spiritual underworld, regret the passing of "Christian America" and the emergence of a religious situation in which the constitutive elements are religious liberty, voluntaryism, and pluralism. Others, in spite of the warning of Professor Ernst Troeltsch himself, have uncritically applied the church/sect typology to the American scene—to the confusion of concerned Christians.

The American churches, however, are neither "church" in the old sense of a state-church Christendom, nor are they "sect." They are a third type: Free Churches in a free society. The liberty of persons of faith to free exercise of religion is matched by the gradual retirement of government from ultimate authority over conscience. "Secular" government is a necessary corollary to Free Churches, a necessary function of religious liberty.

No true church, however, can fail to proclaim the Lordship of Jesus Christ over all of life. No church theologically sound can agree to fence off certain areas ruled by other lords, governed by other loyalties. The American churches, to the degree that they are communities of faithful people, are therefore faced with a dilemma: they can neither continue to use the language and style of established religion, nor can they retreat into the sectarian isolation of earlier dissent from Christendom.

The American churches are thus forced to find a new path, to develop a new style, to function in a new way in the forming of public opinion. This book is an effort to point out some of the implications of the problem, and to indicate the way which believing Christians in America must go. They can neither retreat to the old monolith of Christendom nor can they accept the marginal role of sects.

Appropriate to a work dealing with real problems, and not merely theoretical speculations, some of the interpretations here published have been previously elaborated in seminary and university lectureships, and in articles published in Christian journals. I am grateful to those who have granted such moments of testing to the ideas here developed.

If this work serves to disabuse readers of the notion that American Christianity is nothing but an extension of the thought and style of European Christendom, it will have served a useful purpose. If beyond that it helps to eliminate use of the pejorative terms "sect" and "sectarianism" in reference to the uniquely American experiment in religious liberty, additional gain may be counted. If it inspires concerned writers and scholars to work further along the path of discovery of a new identity for the churches in the American setting, it will fully have achieved the goal set for it.

The book is written and published in the cross-fire of the dialogue with the past and the demands of Christian statesmanship today. It is not written for the balcony but for the arena. At the same time, it is presented in full conviction that we have a unique heritage, a unique potential, and a God-given opportunity for service and witness—*if* we can get our heads screwed on straight as to the nature of the situation in which we have been called to work. Away, then, with longing for the past. Away, too, with retreat from the present. God has yet other pentecosts in store for His church—apostolic, united, disciplined, and renewed.

F. H. L.

Mount Pleasant, Iowa
July, 1968

▶ CONTENTS

THE
CHURCH
AND THE
BODY
POLITIC

▶ I
WHY
ARE
WE
CONFUSED?

AMERICA is experiencing simultaneously two major religious crises. In one of them we have been delayed beyond developments in Europe, where the transition to a new religious situation is completed in all but its outward and legal forms. This crisis is the end of the nineteenth century mood, mentality, and style of churchmanship. We could, of course, adopt another periodization. We might, following Walter Prescott Webb,[1] begin the story of the religious—and the economic and political—expansion of the West at an earlier date. Yet it was the nineteenth century which saw the heyday of "Christian Europe," that culmination of the process of harmonization of religious and ethnic norms and ideals which we identify in Victorian England and the *Wilhelminischen Zeitalter* in Germany. The result of that idealistic harmonism was a continuum, divided to be sure according to ethnic, linguistic, and national blocs, in which little effective distinction was made between Christian imperatives and national self-interest. Moreover, it was fortified against all rebellious movements on the part of the disinherited but increasingly self-conscious masses of people. The instrument of suppression was from 1815 to 1914 a false *oikumene,* a Holy Alliance of Orthodox Russia, Catholic Austria, and Lutheran Prussia. The presuppositions and the goals of this Holy Alliance of religious and political reaction remained relatively intact from the time of the Congress of Vienna (1815) to the destruction of "Christian Europe" in World War I. It was World War I which ended the nineteenth century in Europe, and it also marked there the termination of "Christendom" as a working hypothesis. In America, the changeover to a new religious situation is just beginning to be noticed.

In Europe, the nineteenth century came to an end in two world wars, two depressions, two totalitarian systems. It is no longer possible, except for public-relations purposes, to speak in Europe with the old expansive assuredness of "Christian civilization," "Christian nation," "Christian politics." In America, however, the spirit of manifest destiny has hung on longer, and "Christian America" still seems to some a viable image. Even the great statesmen of missions—although they usually acted on the practical assumption that North America was missionary territory like Asia or Africa—in myth perpetuated the self-image of America as an adjunct of European Christendom. Writing as late as 1926, Robert E. Speer put it this way:

In Great Britain and the United States the State is Christian in theory and principle.

Christ is and has a right to be acknowledged as the head of the State, and all the acts of the State ought to be in conformity with the law of Christianity.[2]

Only with the rise of the "theology of crisis" among the intellectuals, and with the impact of the significance of the election of 1960 upon the national mind as a whole, have the old assumptions been shaken in America.

We are now coming to realize, slowly and painfully, that America is a pluralistic society with a "secular" government. The legal situation changed earlier. The constitutional foundation was changed when, with the adoption of the First Amendment to the federal Constitution (1789–91), America entered upon the unique experiment of religious liberty and voluntaryism. But only in the last few years, with the end of Protestant and white Anglo-Saxon dominance, have the courts and the people as a whole accepted pluralism as normal.

Acceptance of pluralism requires fundamental changes in the different self-images of the religious communities. It affects the nature and style of public pronouncements and the actions by religious bodies. It changes the function and form of the Christian college and seminary. It impels a new and different language in the civic forum. Above all, it means that religious bodies can no longer depend upon governmental patterns and structures to provide the models, the support, and the channels for effecting Christian purposes. The churches cannot expect the government any longer to establish Christianity for them, to provide the outward limits and forms which give them order and defined status. The churches must become vertebrate, backing their words and actions by internal discipline. The religious optimism directed to government, schools, public welfare agencies, medical centers and profession, as instruments for effecting Christian ends, can no longer be justified. A new theology is imperative.

The second crisis, shared with Western Europe, and with

Communist Eastern Europe at a different level, is the end of "Christendom" itself. This issue runs deeper than the end of nineteenth-century optimism and expansionism: it involves the whole complex of relationships by which the church has been related to state and society since the foundations were laid a millennium and a half ago by Constantine, Theodosius, and Justinian. On the Continent, among the younger Catholic and Protestant theologians, the expression "the end of the Constantinian era" is common. American theologians are beginning to get the point, half reluctantly. In America, a very brilliant and biting discussion of the implications of the end of Christian dominance for the Christian-Jewish dialogue has been published by a rabbi.[3] According to him, in the murderous rebellion and apostasy of millions of "Christians" baptized under Hitler, with the resulting massacre of European Jewry, the death-knell for Christendom was sounded.

However that may be, in the sweep of Communism across two-thirds of the world's peoples, with whole sections of Christendom being torn away and more and more lands closed to the missionary preaching and teaching of the gospel, a climax has been reached in history which extends far beyond the trauma of the Third Reich. The viability of the concept of Christendom was first shaken by the treason of the baptized against the Head of the Church. It has been shattered finally with the collapse of the cultural fortress of Western Europe, which was for centuries the base for the religion's status and authority across the world map.

Yet the patterns of thought hold on, crippling missions in the newer nations and muting and muffling the thought and action of believing men and women where they are still found in the old world. Resistance to indigenization by the Younger

Churches is almost as damaging to the future of the faith as the existence of so-called "Christian" political parties in the so-called "Christian" nations. In Europe, nothing is more corrupting to sound international relations than the false image of an intact "Christendom" in the West confronting an "atheistic Communist" bloc in the East. The truth is that both West and East are materialistic and polytheistic and— speaking in traditional language—"missionary territory"; the peril is that when a hard materialism confronts a soft materialism, the hard materialism will conquer every time.

Nothing is more misleading to a vigorous facing of the alternatives than the notion that the nations from Scandinavia to the Iberian Peninsula are still "Christian" in some meaningful sense of the word. In Sweden, although over 98 per cent are officially counted by the Lutheran state church, less than 4 per cent are in effective connection. In Italy, although over 99 per cent are officially counted by the Roman Catholic establishment, less than 12 per cent of the men go to one confession and one communion a year. No self-studies have been made in Spain or Portugal, but the claim of these nations to be "Christian" need hardly be discussed.

The base of Christian missions, and much of the spiritual and intellectual energy of the Christian movement, has already shifted westward to North America and outward to the Younger Churches. In fact, if soundness of verbal confession and purity of life are any test of Christianity, the compelling evidences are to be found today in such congregations as those of the Kikuyus of Kenya or the Fiji Islanders. The Younger Churches are far more "Christian" than old Christendom remains. The basic forms of European theology and church life were given during the centuries when, pressed by an insurgent Islam on the south and subject to the hazards of barbarian raids from the north and east, the theologians and hierarchs of the area dedicated themselves to building and holding a fortress. In the nineteenth century some inner mellowing occurred, and the persecution of dissenters and Jews flagged. But Christianity will not become a major force in European society again until the churches there accept the necessity for disestablishment, and begin to enjoy the benefits of voluntary religion and secular government.

The last savage irruption of baptized heathenism in the area has already alienated many of the most intelligent and sensitive spirits, and rendered the Christian cause incredible to millions around the world. In Rolf Hochhuth's morality play, *The Deputy,* Act Five is entitled, "Auschwitz, or Where are You, God?" In Scene One, a young girl herded toward the crematorium, in the midst of her monologue, reflects, "Cold, God is cold; my hands grow numb when I try to fold them to pray with." [4]

In André Schwarz-Bart's *The Last of the Just,* the solitary just man is comforting the children at Drancy (the gathering point for deportation of Jews in Vichy France). As they are herded toward the freight car which will be sealed to transport them to the gas chambers in extermination camps in Eastern Europe, he promises, "When we reach the Kingdom of Israel. . . ." The tale continues:

Suddenly the doctor's arid, ravaged face was close to his own. "What are you doing?" she whispered in his ear while the children retreated in fear. Ernie looked down and discovered that the living corpse he was rocking had become a dead corpse. The doctor clutched at his shoulder; her fingernails dug into what remained of Ernie's flesh. "How can you tell them it's only a dream?" she breathed, hate in her voice.

Rocking the child mechanically, Ernie gave way to dry sobs. "Madame," he said finally, "there is no room for truth here." [5]

"There is no room for truth here." This is precisely the truth which has led in our time to ecstatic utterance concerning the "death of God."

Behold a bishop in Atlanta, who never once in six years of decisive national and international events uttered a pastoral word to help his men or his people come to terms with the May 17, 1954, decision against racial segregation in the public schools. And now, outside the ghettos of the pious, the ground is stained with the blood of Medgar Evers, Michael Schwerner, Viola Liuzzo, Jon Daniels, James Reeb, James Jackson and others, and their known murderers walk the jungle paths in unchallenged arrogance. Truly, here is an authority on the "death of God"!

Behold two bishops, one in Atlanta and one in Los Angeles, so anxious for God's future and so uncertain about the nature of dialogue on campus, as to agree simultaneously that there is no place on a university campus for a man who challenges the familiar form of words of a faith. "They ought to be ashamed to take money from Christian institutions for their salaries," pontificated one, in referring to the Young Turks in the group.[6] And the other, reminded that Dr. Thomas J. J. Altizer of Emory University had tenure, is reported to have lamented, "That's part of the problem." [7] Is it too much to mention the fact that in educated circles it is customary to read authors' writings, and not to judge them on the basis of *Time* magazine[8] or other secondary sources? Is it still too early for the truth to have penetrated some parts of the church that Truth is best served by full, free, and informed discussion and not by scandalous attacks on persons? No wonder so many of our great universities have found it necessary, over the years, on reaching maturity to sever connections

with the denomination in order to protect the dialogue and
the service to Truth.

The rejoinder of the critics to the champions of verbal
orthodoxy is appropriate and soundly biblical: "Where then
is your god?" "Cry aloud: for he is a god; either he is talking,
or he is pursuing, or he is in a journey, or peradventure he
sleepeth, and must be awaked!" (I Kings 18:27.) The effect of
the various spokesmen for the "death of God" group has been,
although each intends something much more radical and
substantive, to raise the question of how fully the sometime
defenders of traditional views are entitled to presume to
speak for God. In many cases the verbal protests scarcely
mask the hidden atheism of the spokesman.

We are confused and we are distracted by false prophets
using the language of a bygone age, and we are unable to respond creatively to the challenge of the voices of "ecstatic
utterance"—who signalize in fact a resurgence of the spirit of
prophecy in the midst of archaic forms and instruments—
because our self-understanding is out of touch with reality.
The most embittered effort to enforce "values" and "order"
by the methods of a police state cannot succeed, even if
blessed by nineteenth-century churches devoted to outward
probity and inward unbelief. The most resolute determination to continue America as a spiritual peninsula of European
Christendom will fail, for "Christendom" is in Europe a
stinking corpse upon which fascist vultures feed, and in
America the new intellectual and spiritual life flows toward
pluralism, the dialogue, and liberty of conscience.

The challenge of religious liberty, that most precious of
all our liberties in America, is twofold: to build up religious
communities known for their disciplined life and service,
and to build up a secular society noted for the respect paid

the liberty and dignity and integrity of every human person in it. The faithful community serves the One whose Name is known: the sons and daughters of the stranger, men of good will, serve even though they know not the name of the "Incognito Christ." To the time and place of transition it is necessary to look beyond the walls of the fortress to identify the servants of God.

In America, as in Europe, "Christendom" has come to an end. What shall replace it is not, however, the same in both areas. Europe is apparently caught up in a "post-Christian" as well as "post-Constantinian" situation. In America, for reasons to be laid out, the situation is, if anything, "pre-Christian." It would be a fatal mistake to confuse the two histories any longer: in America, the actual effect of the ecstatic utterance of critics has been to purify Christian teaching and practice; in Europe, the ablest critics are generally in the opposition camps.

▶2
THE THREE PERIODS OF AMERICAN CHURCH HISTORY

SPANISH Catholicism was planted in areas contained in the present United States before English colonization, but this fact did not shape the national consciousness in the early period. American church history may be divided into three periods, each with characteristic movements and personalities, and the first period was dominated by British Christendom. From 1607 until well into the nineteenth century, which is more than half of our self-conscious history, the relations between Christianity and culture, church and state, were with minor and fleeting exceptions precisely those which characterized the homeland. Just as the governments of the fourteen colonies—Nova Scotia did not revolt but must be reckoned with the other thirteen until after the Revolutionary War—were but extensions of British sovereignty, in one form or another, the dominant pattern of church life, too, was like a mirror held to religion in the mother country.

When church historians finally emerge from the protectionist stance in which denominational and apologetic interests presently surround them, they will certainly follow the political, economic, and military historians to Europe and reconstruct the religious history of the colonial period from that vantage point. Up to a generation ago the professors of American history were still writing filial history, looking back through the long tunnel to forces but dimly perceived and often unintelligible from the inside. There then arose a generation which went to London, to the archives of the Colonial Office. In the not too distant future practitioners of American church history, still a neglected discipline even in the seminaries, will study the first period where the most important sources and the one vantage point may be found: in the files of the Bishop of London and the home offices of the Society for the Propagation of the Gospel and the Society for the Promotion of Christian Knowledge. This may sound like a point of interest only to special students of church history, but it is not. As we shall see, one of the most dangerously false images burdening American Protestants goes back to a gross misunderstanding of the place of religion in colonial America.

In the first period, to repeat the summary statement, American religion was an extension of British Christendom. Up to 1820, 85 per cent of the population was British in origin. Up to 1834, a state church of the British type enjoyed special privileges in the strongest of the northern colonies, Massachusetts. In New Hampshire, Catholics were discriminated against at law until 1876, and Jews until 1912. The

"Christendom" which characterized more than half of our history was not only present: it was dominant here exclusively and blindly. Religion in colonial America, the religion of the Founding Fathers, was predominantly British, Protestant, and coercive in style!

Established religion was suppressive and intended to be such. In 1674 Governor Berkeley of Virginia was asked by the Home Office, "What course is taken about instructing the people within your government in the Christian religion?" (Note the assumption of governmental responsibility.) He replied, and we may assume that as a colonial functionary he had some instinct for what views would be gladly heard at home:

> The same course that is taken in England, out of town: every man according to his ability instructing his children. But I thank God that there are no free schools nor printing, and I hope we shall not have them in a hundred years; for learning has brought disobedience and heresy and sects in the world, and printing has divulged them and libels against the best of governments. God keep us from both.[1]

For a long time both free religion and public education were, in fact, kept out of Virginia.

The second period of American church history, which overlaps the first period and in some places the third, may be said to have begun with the Great Awakening. The first Great Awakening, beginning in 1734 and 1735 in New England and the Middle Colonies, and continuing in Virginia through to the Revolution, first brought to the fore a principle that was to have enormous influence to the present day: religious affection and affiliation are rightly conceived as voluntary. Preaching which appealed for personal decision first exposed the inconsistencies of the New England standing order, its theology and its government. It was voluntary participation and support which made religious liberty a workable alternative to the state church system. It was, as Timothy L. Smith has conclusively shown,[2] mass evangelism that launched and impelled the first social crusades which gave American Protestantism its characteristic image. It was the approach to America as a mission field which, uniting home missons and foreign missions in a common universal platform, gave our churches that world-mindedness and cooperative attitude often commented on admiringly by European churchmen. In the American hope of things to come, the gathering in of the nations and the reunion of the churches have shared the spotlight of the Christian vision and prayers for generations.

The first period of American church history was dominated by the New England way and the Anglican establishments to the west and south. There was Congregationalist initiative, represented by such men as Lyman Beecher, Charles C. Finney, Henry Ward Beecher, and the lay evangelist Dwight L. Moody. And the magnificent record of organs like the American Board of Commissioners for Foreign Missions and the American Missionary Association should be mentioned. Revivalism in the New England line tended also to produce perfectionist and communitarian manifestations such as the Oneida Community, the Oberlin School, the Kingdom of Deseret—as well as to express itself in social crusades such as abolitionism, peace, temperance, prison reform, Chicago Commons. There was a Presbyterian initiative, especially important at the time of the constitutional conventions and the launching of the new republic. The Presbyterian system had great difficulty, however, in adapting itself to revivalism and mass evangelism: numerous divisions occurred and new denominations were founded as a result of conflict over the relationship of personal experience to Calvinist confessions of faith, over the use of preachers without formal training, over many other problems which arose in relating a traditional covenant theology and order to voluntaryism. The great revival churches, the churches which owe their very existence as major movements to successful home missions, were the Baptists, the Methodists, and the Disciples. These three were the most successful movements of the second period. In many sections these have become for all practical purposes the established churches, and theirs is the characteristic style of nineteenth-century American Protestantism.

Between the second and third periods of American religious history there is, again, considerable overlay. There is good evidence that the nineteenth-century continuum of religious and cultural values, which came to an end in Europe during World War I, still controls important centers of power in the theological schools, boards and agencies, and pulpits of our major denominations. In reality, however, the given situation has changed radically. America is no longer a Protestant nation, even formally. It is no longer even a mission field dominated by Protestant revival churches. The United States is becoming a Great City, in which the fundamental present characteristic is a pluralism of religious commitments and a variety of cultural and racial backgrounds.

During the period of history when American Protestantism was being aerated and regenerated by the revivals' stress on voluntaryism and lay initiative, two other developments were taking place which now condition in a major way our religious situation.

In the first place, and within Protestantism, several millions of foreign-language immigrants were coming to these shores to establish major communities. In the old Middle

West, especially, Lutherans of Danish, Finnish, Swedish, Nor-
wegian, and German languages and rituals established themselves. There had been, to be sure, some small foreign-
language communities fairly early in our history—Salz-
burgers, Moravians, Mennonites, Huguenots, Seventh-Day
Adventists, etc.—but they had largely accommodated to the
patterns set by British Christendom. The Evangelical Association and the United Brethren, for example, owed their
existence as churches to the fact that Francis Asbury and his
associates felt the German-language converts in the middle
states needed their own services and preachers. But they
adopted the Methodist order and liturgy, and with the dying
out of the last German-speaking generation have reunited
organically with the Methodist Church. The Germans of
Unierte background (Evangelical and Reformed), who have
contributed such leaders of American Protestantism as the
Niebuhr brothers and sister, Elmer G. Homrighausen, and
Paul Lehmann, have now completed the circuit by joining
in founding the United Church of Christ.

The picture is different, however, with the Lutherans.
Emerging from foreign-language ghettos within the last generation, they have recently begun to contribute in a massive way to the theological and liturgical discussions, to the
growing Protestant-Catholic dialogue, and to the conception
and active expression of Christian stewardship and service
(*diakonia*). From 1910 to 1960, Lutheran membership increased fivefold. With intraconfessional union moving forward rapidly, three of the Lutheran bodies—the United
Lutheran Church, the Evangelical Lutheran Church, and the
Lutheran Church, Missouri Synod—are already among the
top ten Protestant churches in membership. They are third,
after the Baptists and the Methodists, in number of churches.

One branch has the largest Protestant parochial school system in the United States. The National Lutheran Council has become a major force in public life. Coming to the fore precisely at the time when there is widespread ferment as to the nature of the church and the articulation of her mission in a new situation, the contribution of these "late bloomers" is already an important force. What we have here is not so much the adaptation of groups of Continental background to British Christendom as strong communities taking an active role in reshaping the whole stance of Protestant America. The breadth of vision being shown is perhaps symbolized by the fact that a brilliant associate editor of the *Christian Century* belongs to the Missouri Synod, and that the first publication grant of the Concordia-based Foundation for Reformation Research made possible the compilation and publication of a much-needed comprehensive bibliography of Anabaptist-Mennonite materials.

The second development during the same period was the coming to strength of the Roman Catholic and Jewish communities. Although French and Spanish Catholicism were important, particularly in the Christianizing of the American Indians, they played little part in early American self-consciousness. At the time of the Declaration of Independence only some 20,000 Americans were Catholic. In the second half of the nineteenth century, however, millions arrived—and an expanding system of missionary and teaching orders and parochial schools was developed to slow down the leakage to a dominant Protestantism which was earlier manifest. From 1900 to 1950 the increase was 16 million; today a membership of over 46 million is claimed. Admittedly, the Catholic system of reckoning church membership is different from that of the denominations of Free Church tradition.

Nevertheless, Catholic influence in public life—represented by such an excellent agency as the U.S. Catholic Conference, and appropriately symbolized by the election of a member of the Catholic community to the Presidency in 1960—is powerful and growing. The building of a vast system of church schools, from the grades through graduate level, is no mean accomplishment for a communion whose members were often brought here at company expense on dollar-a-day contracts—and that as late as the early years of the twentieth century. A few years ago there was not one man of the over four hundred in the American Catholic hierarchy whose father had a college education! Today there are as many young men training for the priesthood in this country as for all the Protestant ministries. There are excellent periodicals, such as *Commonweal* and *America*; and since the accession of Pope John XXIII the Protestant-Catholic dialogue has broken open in a way where, on many local levels, the Protestants are often hard put to it to match the scholarly and intellectual competence with which the Catholics are prepared to function.

Moreover, American Catholicism—represented by clerics like the late Gustave Weigel and John Courtney Murray, Georges Tavard, Daniel Callahan, Bernard Cooke, John Cronin, and Colman Barry, and by laymen like Dumont Kenny, Thomas O'Dea, John Cogley, Leonard Swidler, Michael Novak, and Matthew Ahmann—is on the threshold of a major intellectual and spiritual renaissance. For over fifty years the chief financial support of the Vatican and its various agencies has come from America. Today American Catholicism is a major intellectual, devotional, and liturgical force in the world. American Catholics are a major force in supplying the missionaries, the priests for retarded areas like

Latin America, and the leadership to rework the Catholic thought in such difficult areas as church-state relations.

American Jewry has become, too, the chief intellectual, cultural, and financial center of Judaism. Although the founding of the state of Israel in 1948 bears somewhat the same relation to the thinking of our Jewish fellow citizens as Rome does to Catholic thought, no substantial number of American Jews has accepted the notion that their citizenship here "in the diaspora" is either transitory or provisional. Israel itself depends to a large extent for its existence, both diplomatic and financial, upon America.

The one plank in Hitler's program which was actually carried out was the most wicked of all: the elimination of European Jewry. And, as occasionally leaks to the outside world, the status of practicing Jews in the Communist area is at least strained and provisional. The major center of Jewish culture and religious practice has come to be the United States. There are many cities in our society where the Jewish congregations and community agencies afford a major, if not *the* major, civilizing force—as a power for civic betterment, for education, and for the suppression of violence and anarchy. There are important centers of Catholic-Protestant dialogue in Switzerland, Germany, and the Netherlands; the center of Christian-Jewish cooperation, and more recently, religious discourse, is the United States. It is extremely important that this fact be kept to the fore during these years, lest the enthusiasm for Catholic-Protestant cooperation and the influence of Communist and/or Muslim propaganda divert attention from the extraordinary worth of Christian-Jewish cooperation in America.

The third period of American church history is, therefore, pluralistic at the start. Protestants, Catholics, and Jews—not to mention substantial and increasingly articulate minorities

of Eastern Orthodox, Mormon, and even representative communities of other high religions such as Islam, Buddhism,
Hinduism, Shinto, Confucianism—are being called upon to
prove that the most radical and difficult of all American experiments can be made to work: the separation of the civil
covenant from the religious covenants. All three of the major
religious traditions which influence our life are called upon
to approach the issue in their strength: none of them needs
to compromise or to concede from weakness. We have never
had "separation of church and state" in America, and we do
not have it now. What we have had, in growing measure since
the launching of the republic, is a developing awareness that
only that service is pleasing to God which is voluntary and
uncoerced, and that the best government is nonideological,
"secular." This principle, the separation of the political from
the religious covenants, has profound theological as well as
political meaning. It is basic to the health of our religious
communities as well as to the good of the political common-
wealth.

IS AMERICA "POST-CHRISTIAN"?

There is a widespread legend, carefully cultivated today
in reactionary circles, that America was once a "Christian
nation" and that in recent generations we have been going
to the dogs. One of the greatest jurists in our history said
early in the nineteenth century that America was a Protestant
nation and Christianity part of the common law of the land.[3]
Probably when Alexander Campbell delivered his famous
sermon on John 3:17, in May of 1850, to the House of Representatives in Washington, D.C.,[4] he was, like most of the
churchmen of that period, operating on that assumption.
Many great Protestant preachers enjoyed in those days the

privilege of preaching to such an official congregation. It seems clear too that most of the great revivalists of the second period of American church history perpetuated—even though they acted on the practical assumption that the American people were unbaptized heathen, mission territory as truly as China, India, or Africa—the notion that was fixed in the two centuries of the state churches: that America was a Christian nation, perhaps the very bulwark of Christian civilization. Daniel Dorchester, whose impressive studies at the end of the "Great Century" afford the basis for an accurate appraisal of the success of the revivals in winning the people back to the churches on a voluntary basis, once expressed the situation with which the century opened as follows: "Under such disadvantages did Christianity commence the work of the present century in the United States, and with such high responsibilities. The question to be decided was, shall this American nation be Christian or infidel?" [5]

Dorchester correctly appraised the generation of the Founding Fathers, where the collapse of the colonial state churches, the love affair with French Jacobinism, and the effects of the years of war combined to mute the force of faith. But he perhaps too readily assumed that the crescendo of successful revivals had accomplished the Christianization of the nation. Truly symbolic is the fact that it was his son who, in the General Conference of 1908, proposed the action which struck down the last effective controls of probationary membership before the door into the Methodist Episcopal Church. Disciplinary standards are characteristic of a church which is consciously missionary and consciously a minority set in a hostile culture. Churches which think of themselves as established legally, or as "having arrived" socially, remove the wall of separation. About the same time, the Methodists, the Baptists, and the Disciples also threw wide the doors to promiscuity of church membership—an action which has compromised their witness ever since. For establishments have their own built-in corrections and critiques, but a Free Church that abandons disciplinary standards has surrendered something basic to its identity.[6]

Actually, Dorchester's statistics were more revealing than his generalizations. As would happen in many lands today were the watered statistics of the established churches to be cast aside in favor of voluntary affiliation, when given a choice of getting in or getting out, the Americans exited the churches en masse. The figures for different years show the low state of affiliation at the turning point toward religious voluntaryism, and they also reveal the tremendous effectiveness of the "new methods"—among which must be counted the Sunday schools, Chautauqua, house-to-house visitation, radio and television preaching (all instruments of mass evangelism), as well as the camp meeting and the "Societies of Inquiry." The success of the system of religious liberty and voluntaryism stands out in the Dorchester studies:

Year	Population Holding Church Membership
1800	6.9%
1850	15.5%
1900	35.7%
1926	50.2%

By the recent census, almost 70 per cent are affiliated, and a recent survey showed that 96 per cent of all Americans four-teen years of age and older claim to be.[7] There are, of course, problems in success; but they are different from the problems of decline and fall.

The legend that America was once a "Christian nation"

would seem to make sense only to those prepared to defend the state church style of operation, even though this concept was fairly common during the period when churchmen were still unclear as to the implications of voluntaryism. The leaders of our spiritual underworld, who seek through Prayer Amendments, religious exercises in the public schools, etc., to reverse the law of liberty and re-establish ceremonial religion, are consistent in their primitivism. They lament the "good old days" and they would like to take us back to coercive religion. In this reactionary line they are—and a number are political fascists as well as religiously retrogressive—just like the Marxists. For Marxist societies are also retrogressive in religious matters, seeking to re-establish sacral society and eliminate the incoherences attending respect for liberty of conscience.

We should not be too surprised when even decent people develop vertigo when the abyss of religious pluralism opens before their feet. After all, the coercive pattern obtained for a millennium and a half of "Christendom," and in some respects we are only beginning to understand the far-reaching consequences of a style of churchmanship where affiliation, attendance, support, and church discipline are—from the standpoint of law—strictly voluntary matters. A more careful and hard-headed reading of the record would suggest that, rather than looking back to a lost Golden Age cast largely in the image of European Christendom, we would do well to realize that the Golden Age of religion in America lies, potentially, directly before us.

At the end of the "Great Century of Christian Missions," most Americans are (like the other products of the missions in Asia, Africa, and the islands of the sea) first-, second-, or at most third-generation Christians. And most of the problems

which confront us—theological incoherence, liturgical care-
lessness, racism, moral lassitude—are the characteristic problems of successful mission fields. We shall understand ourselves better as Christians if we realize that our identity is
now with the other Younger Churches rather than with a
style of church-state relation which, even in Europe, belongs
to a past period of church history.

It may well be that the rising influence of the American
Negroes will help us to purge the false image of our situation.
As James Baldwin has pointed out in an exceedingly significant article, "The American Negro has the great advantage
of having never believed that collection of myths to which
white Americans cling: that their ancestors were all freedom-
loving heroes, that they were born in the greatest country the
world has ever seen." [8] One of the major contributions of
the Negroes to their fellow citizens may be to raise doubt
that the "good old days" of Protestant persecution, inden-
tured servitude, limited suffrage, slavery, concubinage, and a
general illiteracy, were so wonderful after all!

Is America in a "post-Christian era"? Perhaps this expression, so frequently used by sensitive Catholic and Protestant
theologians in Europe, is the only way to describe the situation in Europe. After two generations of war, Nazi and Communist totalitarianism, and the wholesale apostasy of millions
of baptized Christians, both Catholic and Protestant establishments from Scandinavia to the Iberian peninsula are in
desperate circumstances. What they need, as the work of the
men of the *Kirchentag*, Kirk Week, *Le Rassemblement Protestant,* etc., suggests, is precisely what the American state
churches produced at the critical moment when their own
past caught up with them: to develop new methods of mass
evangelism capable of moving and winning persons who had

relapsed into heathenism. Let us therefore cast the romantic legend resolutely aside, and praise the great men who by mass evangelism and home missions shaped a far richer and worthier heritage than we have sometimes had eyes to see and hearts to understand!

The time has come to turn in most areas from mass evangelism to instruction in disciplined witness. This does not mean that mass evangelism should be abandoned. But it does mean that the priority can no longer lie with the mere acquisition of numbers of new members on almost any basis at all. At the opening of the nineteenth century the problem was "infidelism" outside the churches. As we enter the new age of American religion, the problem is "infidelism" within the churches. Some have said that we are in a "post-Protestant era" in the United States, and in a certain sense this is true. A better way to put it, however, would be to say that we are not in a "*post*-Christian era" but in a "*pre*-Christian era." Our true problems are no longer those of "Christendom" in collapse, but of the successful mission field which has not yet matured into a viable and dependable style of life and thought.

The purpose of the interreligious dialogue, of our accepting the voluntaryism which is our heritage and the pluralism which is our situation, is not to obscure basic issues. We are in some public cultic moments already in danger of substituting a kind of Fourth Religion: a civic cult theologically very like the *positives Christentum* of the Nazis or the "progressive religion" of the Communists, in place of expressions of faith which have historical integrity. Martin E. Marty, in *The New Shape of American Religion,* is one who has pointed out the grave dangers of religion-in-general on the American scene.[9] Our turn must not be toward religion-in-general, "militant Christianity" vaguely conceived. Dialogue, like religious liberty, has meaning only among persons who have convictions. In a very real sense, the Protestant contribution to the interreligious dialogue waits on our purging our minds and spirits of false images and our achieving a mature self-knowledge as to who we are, where we are, and what our responsibility to the Lord of nations and generations presently requires. Not less clarity but clearer self-knowledge, including a richer sense of our time and our heritage, is demanded of us.

THE GEOGRAPHY OF AMERICAN RELIGION

At the opening of the period of religious voluntaryism, the Baptists and the Methodists were already at work. Although the Great Awakening is remembered in New England history for Jonathan Edwards' reports and the effect on his theology and professional career, and the successful resistance of the clergy to Whitefield's second mission, its permanent effects may be measured in the emergence of separationist congregations which counted themselves Baptists. C. C. Goen's excellent study of revivalism in New England documents the way in which "Independent Congregationalists," disenchanted with the state church order, shifted finally to the Baptist banner.[10] Baptists were also strong in the South and after 1820 they grew more rapidly there than in New England, for Congregational power remained stronger than Anglicanism after disestablishment. To the south, in Virginia and North Carolina, the Wesleyan movement was especially strong both within the Anglican parishes and in separate societies. The Disciples joined the work of mass evangelism following the Cane Ridge Revival, and added a note which steadily gained acceptance in the camp meetings: that of church unity. Both Methodists and Baptists thought of themselves as cast in the New Testament pattern, and John Wesley believed the avoidance of sectarian disputes to be a mark of primitive Christianity; but it was the particular contribution of the Campbells, father and son, to make the cooperation and eventual reunion of the churches a permanent mark of the revivals. In spite of the delight which many great revivalists took in public disputation, more significant as a continuing phenomenon was their cooperation in the camp meetings and campaigns.

Baptists never grew as rapidly in the northern tier of states as in the South. Congregationalists, for some time in conjunction with the Presbyterians in the Plan of Union (1801–26), maintained a powerful influence as New England culture spread westward across the continent. The Disciples were particularly strong in Ohio, Indiana, Illinois, Kentucky, Tennessee, Missouri, Arkansas, Oklahoma, and Texas. The Baptists in the South, organized in their convention in 1845 and vastly augmented in total numbers by Negro congregations, grew enormously there. Today, two out of five Baptists are Negroes, mainly organized in two large conventions of their own; 80 per cent of Negro Protestants are Baptists.

When we break down religious affiliation by states and counties, something which Edwin Gaustad has assisted us in,[11] we readily perceive how the religious complexion of America has changed across three and a half centuries. In 1650 a high degree of geographical unity was evident: with Congregationalists in New England, Baptists in Rhode Island, Dutch Reformed in New York, Presbyterians on Long Island, Lutherans in Delaware, Anglicans in Virginia. Today the pattern has changed, but in about one-half of the counties in the United States a single church accounts for at least 50 per cent of all the membership. The areas of greatest homogeneity are dominated by four religious groupings, not one of which was pre-eminent in the colonial period: the Mormons, the Baptists, the Lutherans, and the Roman Catholics. Not a single county of New England is Congregationalist and not a county of the coastal southern states is Episcopalian.

1. In Utah, the Mormons account for over 60 per cent of religious preference in every county, for 90 per cent in all but 3, and for 100 per cent in 6. In 21 out of 44 Idaho counties, 4 counties in Wyoming, 4 in Nevada, and 2 in Oregon, the Mormons are pre-eminent.

2. Even apart from Negro Baptist strength, the Baptists lead in the South: Virginia, North Carolina, South Carolina, Georgia (in every county), Alabama, Kentucky, Tennessee, Oklahoma, Texas, Arkansas, and Missouri are all "Baptist territory."

3. The Lutherans predominate in two-thirds of North Dakota's counties, in Nebraska, in South Dakota; in Minnesota and Wisconsin every county is either Lutheran or Catholic.

4. Roman Catholics have over 90 per cent of the church membership in 5 Louisiana parishes and in 6 "valley" counties in Texas. In New Mexico all counties but 5 are predominantly Catholic, in Arizona all but 2, in California every county. In the East, Catholicism predominates in Maine, in every county but Nantucket Island in Massachusetts, in New Hampshire (all but one), in Vermont (all but one), in Connecticut and Rhode Island (every county).

Although they have scattered concentrations, the Methodists—who a century ago numbered 1 out of 5 American church members—are diffused throughout the whole country. Although they count themselves the largest Protestant denomination, they are losing ground in the population increase. The Episcopalians, Presbyterians, and Congregationalists are similarly scattered. The Disciples, having added Georgia, Pennsylvania, West Virginia, Michigan, Nebraska, Washington, Oregon, and California to the states of their heavy concentration in earlier days, are also widely spread across the country. In short, with the exception of the Baptists—who seem by sheer statistical weight to predominate in a number of states—the churches in control during the colonial period or which came to strength during the time of the great revivals are rather generally scattered throughout the nation. Equally important, however, is the fact that the American southeastern states comprise the largest body of intact Protestant culture left in the world. (The whole heartland of the Reformation is now in Communist hands.) And the Southeast is the section of America where industrialism has come latest. It is perhaps natural that the people of that section should be most attracted by the legend that the whole American republic was once rural, white, and Protestant.

CHILDREN OF THE REVIVALS

All Americans are debtors to the great awakenings of religion which made the pattern of religious liberty, and the voluntary initiative which sustains it, a viable principle in our society. We can scarcely imagine how radical a principle was the separation of the political from the religious covenants when it was first mooted, although we gain some sense of it when we hear the anxiety of European brethren where they contemplate disestablishment. Great and good men, like George Washington and Patrick Henry, opposed the Virginia Bill of Religious Freedom: they did not believe that a society could be held together without an established church.

But the group led by James Madison, supported by the leaders of the Great Awakening in Virginia, carried the day. As Madison said, "During almost fifteen centuries, has the legal establishment of Christianity been on trial. What have been its fruits? . . . Pride and indolence in the clergy, ignorance and servility in the laity: in both, superstition, and bigotry, and persecution." [12]

It is a fact for which we may be profoundly grateful that disestablishment in America came at the hands of men who loved the Church, and was encouraged by evangelists who had demonstrated that a people could be brought to assume the obligations of religion by the power of the Spirit rather than by the requirements of law, instead of as a result of anticlerical agitation. We have never had a significant anticlerical tradition in America: militant anticlericalism is a typical by-product of the coercion of the spirit by established churches.

But religious liberty will not function in a society which has grown indifferent to the claims of religion. When a spiritual vacuum is created, where members are relaxed and undisciplined, seven ideological devils rush in. The genius of our tradition has been pedestrian politics and enthusiastic religion, problem-solving politics and mission-minded, eschatologically oriented faith. In post-Christian situations, politics has become exciting and religion deadly dull. Where the Nazi and Communist ideologies have emerged to strength, they have replaced an ill-defined and static culture-religion. It is cause for considerable reflection that we are beginning to see the emergence of eschatological politics in America, and it raises serious questions as to the quality of disciplined and sacrificial faith being developed in our churches. In some areas the lovely Christian ladies who once saved pennies for missions and collected supplies for the outposts among tribes not yet gathered into the fold have been superseded by little old women in tennis shoes who exude anxiety and live in soundproof rooms, apparently surrounded by apparitions: a President, a Supreme Court, a National Council of Churches, a United Nations, all controlled by "devils." We are not expecting enough of church members. Widespread indiscipline is beginning to produce not just apathy but wickedness. Is the Free Church, whose discipline and energetic purpose were so essential to the health of the open society, being replaced by low-demand culture-religion, socially if not legally, of the order of establishment?

This brings us to the most serious crisis confronting the American Protestant churches, the problem to which every other issue returns: the loss of membership standards, both probationary and full. The tremendous statistical success of the second period of our church history, which brought into the church more "new Christians" than were gained in any other time or place in two thousand years, and for which we should thank God daily, was accompanied by the virtual elimination of standards of membership. Among the great revival churches the fateful transition can be marked on the calendar with considerable precision. The trauma of the Civil War, when churches both north and south identified with sectional interest in reckless abandon, marked the beginning of the slide into acculturation. The process was completed around the turn of the century, when Methodists and Baptists and Disciples more or less openly ceased to exercise church discipline.

Church discipline, which sounds so negative to us today, was a great affirmation in the development of the Anabaptist radical Puritan Free Church testimony. In matters of faith, decision was no longer to be given by princes or town councils or lords of manor, but to be determined by the whole body of the faithful under the guidance of the Holy Spirit. The pioneer Free Churchmen were not just opposed to persecution in religious matters, which could under no circumstances "be harmonized with the Spirit, doctrine, and conduct of Christ." [13] Rather, they were concerned for the restoration of the apostolic principle of decision-making:

> I would say further, if the magistrates rightly understood Christ and His Kingdom, they would in my opinion rather choose death than to meddle with their worldly power and sword in spiritual matters which are reserved not to the judgment of man but to the judgment of the Great and Almighty God alone.[14]

Religious liberty was not affirmed by its early martyrs because it was good for society or because it made a better government, although these were secondary benefits not to be despised. It was affirmed because only in this way could Christians attain to that level of disciplined witness which the Head of the Church expected of His people.

The liberty of the Christians is obedience to God in Christ and submission to the governance of God the Holy Spirit. But if they grow lazy and disobedient wherein is their claim to freedom from outside control?

The *form* of freedom is this: to be able to decide for one's self.

The *secret* of freedom is this: to be without anxiety for one's self.

And the *meaning* of freedom is this: Love.[15]

We Protestants are entering the third period of American church history with love in short supply. We are often anxious (but see I John 4:18). We are often resentful of the winsomeness of the alternatives to the evangelical faith. What we urgently need is a new outpouring of that faith which won a continent, grounded in that confidence which Philip Schaff expressed in the last year of his life: "The Reformation of the 16th century is by no means the last word which God has spoken to His people. He has other and greater Pentecosts in store." [16]

Neither was the colonial period, nor the time of the proclamation of religious liberty, the last word. The work of Christianizing the continent is not finished, but well begun. If His people today again respond with appropriate "new methods" of evangelism and disciplined witness, fitted to the needs of our age, we shall see in the years directly ahead one of the major times of renewal in the history of the church. To underline the point: *the Golden Age lies not in the past but, potentially, directly before us.*

3
THE FUTURE OF THE AMERICAN WORLD CITY

THE religious experience of America has not been a simple and continuous development, with no dramatic breaks or sudden turnings. There have been at least two major frontier-crossings of fundamental order: the first, the shift from state churches to the principle of voluntary support; the second, the acceptance of former religious minorities as full-fledged partners in the public dialogue. American Nativists, from the National States' Rights Party to Protestants and Other Americans United ("the college man's KKK"), still do not accept the verdict of history. They attack the Supreme Court for defending the civil rights of minorities and they defame and slander movements like the National Council of Churches and the National Conference of Christians and Jews for advocating open-faced discussion, understanding, and cooperation between religious communities. The kind of Catholic-Protestant dialogue which has developed since Vatican II especially arouses their fury. But history has passed them by, although in their dying throes they may manage to do considerable temporary damage.

The third period of American church history, the Age of Pluralism, is also the Age of Dialogue. For the life of liberty is the life of free, full, and informed discussion. The simple solutions which were possible under an officially monolithic system, in a small and preindustrial country, are no longer faithful answers to the questions put to this nation today. New answers must be discovered, in many cases by courageous experiments and model-building. In the discovery of working models, and in deciding the social policy based upon them, all persons who must live with the results are entitled to share in making the decisions. This is one of the great works of Christ in history—to extend the dignity and honor accorded every member of the religious covenant to every human person in the political covenant. This was the way in which the Church Meeting prepared the way for the Town Meeting, and the same spirit and service informs the great encyclicals *Mater et Magistra* and *Pacem in Terris*. The same creative spirit must inform the churches' service to the society in America today.

THE HISTORICAL SETTING

The major crossing-over which now confronts us as a nation, to the securing of which the work of the churches is imperative, is the achievement of first-class citizenship for all our citizens. Sometimes this is called "the crisis of race," but race is not the fundamental issue. Fundamental is the question whether our constitutional system, with its balance of liberties and responsibilities, shall be extended to all persons within our borders, or whether we shall through insensibility and cruelty toward poor and disinherited minorities be broken on the wheel of history. Grown to a large and enormously wealthy nation, we have now been brought to this frontier of decision, this bar of judgment.

In 1620, the year after the first African slaves reached Virginia, there were still only 2,300 settlers in all.

In 1720, three years after John Wise of Ipswich published his great apology for democratic government, the population was a modest 466,000.

In 1790, as the federal Constitution was being ratified and the Bill of Rights established, Americans numbered almost 4,000,000.

In 1860, as Abraham Lincoln was elected a minority candidate, we counted but 31,443,000. (From 1790 to 1864, of course, slaves counted but three-fifths of a person for census purposes.)

Today, we are well past the 200 million mark. In fact, recently we were startled to read in the newspapers that a scholarly critique of the 1960 census would indicate that total figures at that time were approximately 5 million short of accuracy. While we slept, as it were, the United States passed the magic number of 200 million citizens. Moreover, we are getting younger. By 1970, it is estimated, half of the American people will be under twenty-five. It is difficult for Americans to think historically, for as a people we have been prevailingly future-oriented. Moreover, when we recall that for half of our population World War II—so vivid an experience to most of the older generations—will be almost as remote as the Civil War or the Revolutionary War, we begin to perceive how studiously the dialogue with the past must be cultivated if we are to maintain continuity at all.

Yet it is precisely this dialogue with the past, this wise appreciation of the covenant between fathers and sons, which can today impart wisdom. For to understand the American experiment in liberty and popular sovereignty, we must keep in mind the fact that, with the exception of little Iceland, we have the oldest form of constitutional government in the North Atlantic community. Every one of the other Western nations has gone through one or more revolutions since the American Revolution. Every other people has been ravaged by invasions and/or social upheavals of major proportions. Every one of those countries which once viewed America— with its catch-all immigration policy, its extreme devotion to liberty, its lack of established religion, its social and economic mobility—as the "member of the class least likely to succeed," has itself passed through fire and disaster.

The thought rushes in upon us that a Constitution which has proved viable for so long—a system of government which has outlived so many kingdoms, empires and despotisms— cannot be as bad as some say that it is. Indeed, one of the main tasks of the day is for citizens of conscience to take a stand against the extremists and detractors of America, those who have lost hope in America, and to affirm a steady confidence in self-government. As a matter of fact, where the law of the land is respected and enforced, where the ideals which have inspired us are still living realities, this "last, best hope of man on earth" is today as capable of handling the problems thrust upon it as it was when the connection with the British throne was first broken. The problem is to dislodge from power those who have lost hope in America and to bring to the fore a leadership that is patriotic and affirmative. There is something fundamentally sick and ripe for cure in a society that has nothing better to offer in leadership on the day after the Newark and Detroit riots than the police state mentality of McClellan, Eastland, and Thurmond.

There was once a time of simplicity, or so it seems now. Until 1820, 85 per cent of the American population was white, Protestant, and descended from the peoples of the British Isles. Of course women could not then vote. In fact suffrage was commonly restricted to landholders. Until the latter part of the nineteenth century, probably not more than 1 out of 20 adults exercised the franchise. Today we have universal suffrage. Today we have Catholics and Jews equally entitled at law, and strong in their religious and community lives. Today we have a pluralism of racial and national origins. But the law of liberty remains as simple as it ever was: the one who would himself be free must learn, from time to time, to look through the eyes of his neighbor. Liberty and self-government cannot be strengthened by people whose only answer is to force a return to some mythological past, to ignore the rights of large numbers of fellow citizens.

RACE: THE MOMENT OF TRUTH

Of all the challenges confronting the realization of the dream of human liberty and dignity, at home or abroad, none is so serious today as that which we meet in race and racism. *Ethnicity in religion is heresy, and racism in politics is treason.* And if religion found its most authentic expressions in the nineteenth century in the language of the *person,* in the twentieth century the language of high religion is *political,* having to do with the structure of law and justice. The crisis is, however, constitutional rather than racial.

Athens fell into confusion, dissension, and ruin because the 1 out of 20 who then enjoyed the blessings of liberty and open dialogue did not know in time to share the good and free life with the majority of bondservants and slaves. In failing to extend freedom to others, they lost their own. In truth, the one who would deny liberty to others is not himself worthy of liberty. America has come to that kind of borderline of history, and the fate of our children and our children's children rests almost solely upon this: whether we shall act in time to guarantee the blessings of American life and the protection of the American flag to all of our people, or whether in the *kairos* of our history we who are privileged shall first disappoint the aspiring dreams of the disinherited and then ourselves be destroyed in the judgment of a righteous God. In 1969 it is late in the day, very late. At a time when the world's masses are yearning to breathe free, America's moral leadership on the world stage is fatally compromised by our indecision and lack of good faith here at home.

The struggle for an orderly and constitutional resolution of the problem of second-class citizenship in America has persisted for more than a century. But now that some of the Negro nationalists are beginning to talk the same violent language as the disloyal whites in the Klu Klux Klan (KKK), the National States' Rights Party, and the John Birch Society, we cannot count indefinitely on the patience of the Negro. After all, there is no denunciation of the American government uttered by Carmichael or Brown that was not long ago made popular by the White Citizens' Councils. There is no disloyalty by leaders of the Communist Party, of no public position, that cannot be matched by the wicked and disloyal behavior of George Wallace, Lester Maddox, James Eastland, and Orville Faubus. Why we should expect young American Negro citizens to submit indefinitely to a crippling of their educational aspirations and political rights to satisfy the prejudices of disloyalists who have not yet accepted the verdict of the American Civil War is a puzzle. Even more perplexing is to see the Republican Party, once led by Abraham Lincoln and patriotic nationalists, sink into the moral swamps of Copperhead politics and appeasement of nullification of the federal Constitution.

The political record which has brought the American Negro to despair and revolt is plain enough to read. The 13th, 14th, and 15th Amendments were clear enough, and had the Constitution been loyally enforced, the anguish of our present conflict would long since be dim memories. But America was betrayed, and at high level, not long after Lincoln's martyrdom.

In 1876, in a dishonest deal for the Presidency of the United States, the leaders of the Republican Party bought Louisiana's disputed electoral votes for Rutherford B. Hayes in return for a promise to abandon the attempt to enforce the Constitution in the former Confederate States. By 1880 the decent people in the South, white and black, those who like Robert E. Lee were willing loyally to accept the verdict of the war and build a better America, were squeezed out of power and influence: the filthy and treasonous politics of the KKK, lynch law, and the night-riders took over. In 1883, in a decision as fateful and as morally wrong as the decision in the Dred Scott Case (1857) which made the Civil War inevitable, the Supreme Court threw out the Civil Rights Act of 1875. The betrayal was thus complete, and until the Fair Employment Practices Commission (FEPC) order of 1943 was issued during the exigencies of World War II the Negro citizen remained unprotected at law. He lived without defenders in a social jungle, and all too often those who were sworn to protect the helpless were in fact in league with the

beasts of prey. Much of the resentment of the young Negro
toward "law and order" derives from the fact that for generations his people have been victimized by lawless policemen.
Just as serious for all of us, there operated from 1880 until
1960—with but slight interruption—a backdoor alliance of
reactionaries lodged among northern Republicans and southern Democrats, an alliance which blocked at every turn any
measures proposed to move America along the path of social
progress.

With *the election of John F. Kennedy,* and the shattering
of the myopic dream of an America dominated by white
Anglo-Saxon Protestants, a new moral initiative for the good
of the nation began to emerge. By this time in our national
history, with World War II behind us and the encounter
with totalitarian systems dominating the world scene and
influencing internal politics, men of liberty were coming to
see that liberty is in fact indivisible. Slavery is as debasing to
master as to slave. No nation that loves liberty can endure half
slave and half free, partly first-class and partly second-class
citizens. The conviction grew that those who would deny
liberty and dignity to their fellows were unworthy of an
audience. In the "new South," an economy based on other
structures than colonialism and led in some places by other
types than the Bilbos and the Eastlands began to appear. The
racist bigotry of the Radical Right was discredited and sinking into the pit from which it had emerged. The religious
bigotry of groups like Protestants and Other Americans
United was declining before the powerful upsurge of the will
to brotherhood—signalized by the pioneer efforts of the National Conference of Christians and Jews, and launched at
floodtide by good Pope John and Vatican II.

The high point, the sequence of events which above all
indicated that the sour humours of decades of moral laziness

were being blown away, came in those glorious months from January through August, 1963, when it seemed again that Americans were capable of the moral fervor and disciplined devotion to purpose which marks a great nation. As in the saving of the Union a century before, it was an alliance of spiritual vigor and structured power which gave hope. The power came from cooperation between the great Protestant, Catholic, and Jewish communities which had, in the previous four decades, emerged as associations of social and economic identity. As Herberg and Lenski have shown in their important studies—*Protestant/Catholic/Jew* and *The Religious Factor*[1]—it is imperative to distinguish the power of the faith communities from the function of churches and synagogues, as such. The moral force came from two factors in the renewal movements of the postwar period: (*a*) the will to ecumenical and interfaith dialogue, and (*b*) the plea among the disfranchised and exploited peoples all over the world that they be treated as human persons. As Pope John XXIII put it in his great social encyclical addressed "to all men of good will," *Pacem in Terris* (April 10, 1963), the signs "clearly show that the men of our time have become increasingly conscious of their dignity as human persons." And again:

We see that every man has the right to life, to bodily integrity and to the means which are necessary and suitable for a proper development of life. . . . By the natural law every human being has the right to respect for his person, to his good reputation, the right to freedom in searching for truth and in expressing and communicating his opinions. . . . And he has the right to be informed truthfully about public events.[2]

In America, the moral offensive began with the great National Conference on Religion and Race, held in Chicago in January, 1963.[3] This conference marked the first time in history that all major religious bodies, to the number of seventy-seven, officially cooperated on anything. The Church Federation of Greater Chicago (under the leadership of Dr. Edgar H. S. Chandler), the Chicago Catholic Archdiocese (on the direct initiative of the late Albert Cardinal Meyer), and the Chicago Board of Rabbis were host agencies to the conference. Dozens of state and metropolitan and local conferences organized support for the same cause in the weeks that followed. Hightide was reached in August of that summer, when over 200 thousand Americans of the most varied ethnic, cultural, and religious backgrounds rallied in Washington, D.C., to end second-class citizenship once and for all. Rabbi Joachim Prinz stated at that great rally the problem of atomism and indifference, the twin forces which still impeded the triumph of righteousness. Reactionary politicians and the leaders of our spiritual underworld warned everyone to "get out of Washington—the liberals and the colored are coming!" As a matter of fact, Washington was on that day the safest city in the country, and for several days its crime rate fell off markedly. The rally itself was a pentecost, an outpouring of moral and spiritual conviction which more than any other single event broke the filibuster in Congress that still attempted to perpetuate second-class citizenship for American Negroes. " 'Bigotry and hatred are not the most urgent problem,' he [Prinz] said that day. 'The most urgent, the most shameful problem is silence. America must not remain silent.' " [4]

Looking back, one is appalled by the losses we have suffered and at the extent to which we have been sinking into spiritual confusion and fatalism. Pope John and Cardinal Meyer and President Kennedy and Dr. King are gone from the scene. The Civil Rights Act of 1965 was adjourned without action by a low-level political deal, with Senator Everett Dirksen of Illinois leading the Copperhead compromise; only an upsurge of public indignation saved the 1968 Act from the same fate. The nation has sunk deeper and deeper into the swamps of war in Southeast Asia, in a commitment so shapeless and formless that the best of public opinion is polarized between the demand for a sheerly military solution and the demand for an embarrassed retreat in the face of expanded Communist aggression. With the inner city riots in northern United States, the polarization has increased. There is a clear breaking line between those turning fascist and urging that the police be given greater powers to put down any protests peaceful or violent, and those who still believe that a nation that can spend two and a half billion dollars a month in Vietnam, can make at least a parallel effort to build cities decent enough for Americans to live in.

It is the Vietnam issue that has distracted and destroyed our moral initiative. It is the diversion of the limited energies of church, academic, and civic-minded groups to protest the American commitment in Southeast Asia which has weakened the leadership of the churches here at home. If the moral and political strength which had been marshaled to press forward justice at home had been developed to full advantage, the despair and dismay and disorder of Watts, Newark, Detroit, and a dozen other inner city explosions could have been averted. The Vietnam War has diverted national attention and consumed national energies. There are wise men who believe that the confusion of the two issues—Vietnam and civil rights—has done a profound disservice to sensible discussion of both. Certainly, it must be stated that the situation in Southeast Asia has been ambiguous and susceptible of several loyal and intelligent solutions. Some months ago

Chairman Mao of Red China announced the intention of his followers to promote "five or six Vietnams." His remarks were echoed by one of Castro's agents in Latin America. In the same meeting in Havana at which Stokely Carmichael denounced his country, the slogan of "five or six Vietnams" was again raised.

This is the real weakness of so many of the slogans proclaimed by well-meaning, peace-loving members of the campus and church communities. If we retreat in Southeast Asia, where shall we make a stand? If we "negotiate now!" with whom shall we negotiate? At the next opportunity—as the Russian June, 1967, "probing" in the Near East clearly showed—the Communists will spare no expense and shun no risk to launch "another Vietnam."

The problem is that we are in that area face to face with an adversary who does not contemplate compromise or negotiation. His politics are ideological, and he is perfectly willing to see a whole nation destroyed before he will yield his "true beliefs." Whatever the abstract arguments, policy is thereby reduced to the level of decision in another and more famous encounter:

> Whom reason hath equald
> Force hath made supream.
> Milton, *Paradise Lost*

This is not the situation concerning internal policy, where —with the exception of small extremist groups—a genuine public consensus existed, and still exists. To the great damage of the common good, and to the jeopardy of the whole system of self-government, many of those preaching a reasonable and orderly securing of the rights and liberties of all American citizens have felt morally obligated to switch their enthusiasms and efforts elsewhere.

We have done wrong to be diverted. The Vietnam issue has been the albatross about the neck of the Johnson administration, the churchmen's public policy, and the entire effort to create a beautiful and just America. Even among the people of the new nations in Asia and Africa, America's handling of the internal issue of racial justice is regarded as her Moment of Truth. Among Communists and fellow travelers on the one hand, and pacifists and isolationists on the other—just as among those who are nationalists overseas and separatists or racists at home—the Vietnam issue has been overriding. Among those who, at home and abroad, long for the victory of a style of government based on popular sovereignty and protection of the rights of every citizen, the priority issue was and remains the constitutional issue symbolized at this time on the matter of racial justice. It is the question of how we resolve the matter of racial pluralism that tests us, in our own eyes and in the eyes of all the new nations. Neither in our churches nor in our cities can we afford to fumble this issue much longer: the time bought for us by Negro moderates, against the shrill demagoguery of white and Negro extremists, has perhaps already run out. One of the most visible straws in the wind is the fact that young Negroes of great ability, although better educated than ever before, are not going into the ministry of the Protestant churches. The seminaries in the American Association of Theological Schools all report the same: the stream which, from Mordecai Johnson and Benjamin Mays to James Farmer and Martin Luther King, Jr., once gave America many of its finest Christian leaders, has virtually dried up in the last few years. The "new Negro" is beginning to turn away from the Protestant church; Mohammed Ali is only the most dramatic sign of it.

However we may judge American intentions in Vietnam, it is clear that we cannot, as a nation, continue that commitment at the expense of major effort at home. The American people, and not just exploited minorities, are giving increasingly clear signs that they are sick of the Vietnam war and what it is doing to us as a nation. It is time for a "rally of Americans"—to deal with the crucial issues that we do know and where our efforts have a chance of meaningful success.

THE AMERICAN EXPERIMENT IN LIBERTY AND SELF-GOVERNMENT

No other people in history has ever attempted an experiment like America. It has always been assumed that an established religion and uniformity of cultic practice were essential to hold a people together: we are attempting religious liberty, pluralism, voluntaryism, and the vitality of the dialogue. Throughout most of human history, racial purity has been considered normative, and lesser and weaker tribes were destroyed or assimilated: in America, although the theory of the "melting pot" was once juxtaposed to the pseudo-scientific racism of Lathrop Stoddard and Madison Grant, we are maintaining a complex of subcultures within the national covenant. It was once assumed that the state, blended with an established church, could lay claim to ultimate loyalties. The totalitarian parties and systems, with their rigid ideologies, still make such claims over conscience. But we are attempting something unheard of: "secular" governments, human inventions to achieve specific goals, limited in scope, theologically speaking "creaturely." The government which knows itself to be a "creature," which makes no ultimate claims, which asserts no final demands over conscience, is a blessing so vast that we scarcely know how to live with it.

It was once assumed that colleges and universities in order to serve Christ must be directly controlled by the church: although there is foot-faulting at some campuses, we are coming to perceive that the Republic of Learning has an integrity, a dignity, and a liberty of its own. We still have among us retrogressive voices who seek to direct us backward into the old style of sacral society, where one religion or creed controlled the public liturgy, the public schools, the universities, social welfare—and all the institutions which have been freed and have acquired a liberty and dignity of their own. Most important of all, it was once assumed—in Christendom as well as in political affairs—that the common folk were at their best when silent, docile, and obedient. This assumption, if we exclude yelling mobs, still rules governmental theories in Russia, China, Spain, Portugal, Poland, South Africa, Angola, North Korea, Egypt, Saudi Arabia, Greece, and a host of other areas over which the clouds of old-style or new-style tyranny lower. These areas have subjects, not citizens. In America, by contrast, we are coming to see that every man and woman is entitled to have a share in making the decisions which govern his destiny. This is precisely the meaning of the Supreme Court decisions enforcing more equitable representation, popularly called "one man, one vote." And, contrary to those who fear the people and distrust liberty, popular sovereignty goes hand in hand with a larger and nobler view of the worth of every person.

The truth is that we have advanced far beyond mere national identity. Our social patterns can no longer be discussed in terms of the urban-rural split of another time. Our corn growers and hog growers and wheat ranchers are just as much a basic part of the highly complex industrial society which America has become as are the men on the automobile assembly lines in Dearborn or the steel mills in Bessemer, Alabama. We are all, whatever our vocation or profession or social role, caught up in a new kind of technical, compartmentalized society. America is becoming the new World City, the place where, for the first time in history, men of the most varied racial, religious, cultural, and linguistic backgrounds are to learn to live together and govern their mutual affairs in mutual respect.

THE ART AND WISDOM OF
COMMUNICATION

For the American experiment to progress further, there must be genuine communication, honest and open-faced encounter, basic dialogue. There are those among us, of course, who deliberately and consistently violate the rules of civilized living—Communists, John Birchers, and their fellow travelers. They broadcast loud and long from soundproof rooms. They never hear a word anyone else says, living in their closed systems of anxiety and hatred. Toward them, with their attack on the churches, we do best to hold to the frequent New Testament warning: "Never admit any charge against an elder except on the evidence of two or three witnesses" (I

Tim. 5:19; cf. II Cor. 13:1). But among those who are loyal
to the American experiment in human liberty and dignity,
among those who have not lost confidence in the One who
keeps His promises, the challenge is to cultivate the hearing
ear and plain speaking. Only by such dialogue, embracing all
who share a common destiny, can our political faith be
energized and redeemed. The alternative to the dialogue is
the knife, and the end of the World City. How do we educate
for faith rather than anxiety, for responsible involvement
rather than escape, for attention to justice for others and not
selfishness?

In any serious educational program, one of the major foci
must be the theory and art of communication. What is true
dialogue? How does communication occur in ways other
than verbal or literary—mime, pantomime, etc.? What are
the latest findings in language theory? What are the languages
of mathematics (binomials, computer science, etc.)? How does
an effective citizen report the minutes of a meeting? How
does he contribute to shaping the public opinion, so that he
and his neighbors may not be victimized by the demagogues?
Above all, *how and where does he learn that it is willing
involvement in self-discipline and service to others which
makes his communication credible?*

Such questions go far beyond the technical, and raise the
central issues of life's meaning. We have never known so much
about the technical skills of communicating. What do we
have that is worth submission to serious discussion with our
neighbors? Communication theory leads us to the heart of
wisdom. A sound educational system will center on the pursuit of wisdom as well as the achievement of technical proficiency. The most awful figure of the modern world is, after
all, the technically competent barbarian—the master of

"human engineering" who has no true anthropology, the skilled master of persuasion who has nothing to say and sells his services to the highest bidder, the careful bookkeeper who counted the bodies at Dachau and Teresienstadt and Auschwitz. Far too many of our campuses have become simply mills for skill training, without any center hidden or revealed. And on them, while wisdom languishes, the young go over to inner emigration and outward revolt.

A triumph of technics is found in the frequent incapacity of the technically proficient individual to accept moral involvement. It is still *callous indifference* which has slowed our progress toward the city of brotherhood to a grinding and grudging halt. (Gandhi was once asked what grieved him most. He replied, "The hardness of heart of the educated.") He all too often throws back emotionally to the spectator posture when confronted by a real crisis and challenge. He is right in maintaining an "objectivity" in the use of all relevant sources and opinions while the dialogue is going on. He is wrong in supposing that such "objectivity" is a virtue when the time has come to accept involvement (*engagement*) and to act. Marshall McLuhan has summed up the dilemma in this fashion:

Western man acquired from the technology of literacy the power to act without reacting. The advantages of fragmenting himself in this way are seen in the case of the surgeon who would be quite helpless if he were to become humanly involved in his operation. He acquired the art of carrying out the most dangerous social operations with complete detachment. But our detachment was a posture of noninvolvement. In the electric age, when our nervous system is technologically extended to involve us in the whole of mankind and to incorporate the whole of mankind in us, we necessarily participate, in depth, in the consequences of our every action. It is no longer possible to accept the aloof and dissociated role of the literate Westerner.[5]

In other words, for dialogue to occur, it must be accompanied by the credible act. This is especially the case with race, in the church and in the public life. Without a center to life, without wisdom, learning is mere cunning and artifice and invention. Without brotherhood-love, which is the highest wisdom, communication however technically competent must fail.

A sound educational pattern will restore the educated to the place where they belong: carrying the heaviest fighting in the battle line. The technician may sit on the balcony and describe the destruction of peoples and nations, and make his own small contribution to that destruction, but the one who has located the Center of life will know that His nature and His name is Love. He will not hesitate to count himself, like his Master, expendable for the salvation of the world. And today, in the area of greatest sensitivity—race—America is called to righteousness, to an adventure into the World City which requires the emancipation of many of our past plans and present fears. But the rule of faith remains: we are called to live in liberty. If we do not, the spirit will be taken from us and given to others bearing fruits more worthy of repentance.

In the end, then, the Lord of the Church and the Lord of History are one. And if we purpose a just and beautiful City, we shall be open to cooperation with all of those who come bearing the fruits of justice, righteousness, mercy, and peace —even if they are not now numbered among the baptized. The Christian imperialist, who would live in the world with none but formally orthodox, has missed the glorious liberty which comes from the Logos of God, the hidden Christ. We are freed to act in love toward the Least Brother, whoever he may be, because we know Who it is that purchased for him and for us the World City of the future.

In the end, the Secular City and Jerusalem the Golden will be one. The last age of church history is also the last age of the history of the world, when the perfection once purposed for it shall be restored, when church, community, schools, university shall all come again under His head and do His will.

▶4
THE
AGE
OF
DIALOGUE

NOWHERE is the spirit and discipline of the dialogue more needed than in the effort of the churches to achieve a new self-consciousness and sense of purposeful orientation in a voluntaryistic and pluralistic culture. Many church leaders have not yet accepted the fact that Protestantism is no longer the controlling force in American public life. Especially in the Deep South, the myth of an earlier and happier age is assiduously cultivated. American religious history needs to be demythologized.

Our thinking would be better if we stopped to realize that we must make our choice and stick with it. Either America was once a Christian (i.e., Protestant) nation and has fallen away, in which case we are committed to defending the state church approach; or America was a needy mission field, in which case we praise the imagination and courage of those who developed highly successful new methods of mass evangelism and made voluntaryism work. Which period is nearer to us and more determinative of our style of church life? Which, if you will, is more worthy of praise and imitation— the age of the established churches or the age of the evangelists? In my judgment, contrasting the style of church life in "Christendom" with that of the mass revivals of religion, we have every reason to be thankful for the mass evangelism which made religious liberty, lay initiative, and voluntary membership viable.

We are now entering a third age of American religious history, regardless of how we esteem and distinguish the first two. This is the age in which, with the dismantling of what is left of the old Protestant establishments, we have a whole host of unanswered questions as to the proper role of religion in public life. These questions can best be answered by a lively network of dialogue groups—Catholic and Protestant, Christian and Jewish—rather than by constant reference to ziggurats erected in another time and place. "Christian America!"

> Twas in another country,
> And besides, the wench is dead!

Even the nature of our religious liberty must be more clearly defined. Quite evidently some writers confuse toleration and liberty: others insist that religion must be driven out of public life altogether; others yet prefer to replace the old Protestant establishment with an establishment of "civic faith" or religion-in-general. A growing number—Catholics and Jews as well as Protestants—are coming to understand that the coefficient of a situation of legal parity is not anti-clericalism but voluntaryism:

> An accurate rendition of what the Constitution dictates will, at least, avoid the waste of hopes and resources caused by solutions based upon

tenuous constitutional exegeses and will compel the development of the kind and volume of voluntary support which, in the last analysis, is the only true measure of devotion to religious institutions.[1]

The potentiality released by religious liberty is not to be the enthronement of the ideology of secularism in public life but the freeing of the church to be the church, and the freeing of the created order to fulfill its own direction of liberties and integrities. The style of relationship appropriate between fellow citizens of differing religious commitments is, in an area of liberty, based on the dialogue.

Sociologically, we speak of the American cultural and racial and religious scene as "pluralistic." With reference to the earlier practices of coerced religion, we speak of the principle of affiliation as "voluntaryism." In terms of human relations, and the duty of every person of conscience to communicate with his neighbors, we speak of the third period of American church history as the Age of Dialogue.

THE MEANING OF DIALOGUE

A person who knows something which he feels to be important for his neighbors to know and fails to communicate it is guilty of lack of love. It is *not*, initially, *agreement* which holds society together but *concern*. That is why the person who at a given point of time disagrees most vigorously with us within the community of reference is far preferable to the one behind whose silence lurks a complete indifference to whether we live or die. A society is not held together by apparent agreement, let alone by an outward façade of unanimity. It is held together by a sense of common life and destiny, and for that sense to be lively and creative, the existence of Loyal Opposition is both desirable and useful.

(Loyal Opposition, so central to the genius of our constitutional tradition, is of course utterly different in style and tone of voice from conspiracy and subversion, which have no place in the public forum.)

That is why such a wave of horror swept through the public spirit some time ago when a woman was murdered at night on a street in Queens, New York City, and thirty-seven witnesses failed to call the police. It took thirty-five minutes and three stabbings for the act to be accomplished, and each of those who remained a spectator and failed to act became—theologically, at least, and probably legally as well—an accomplice. Most of the witnesses, in trying to explain their inaction, said they "did not want to get involved." [2] Like the Dallas citizen, whose moving statement on the price of indifference to hatred and organized viciousness was published in *Look*[3] after the assassination of the President, the witnesses didn't want to get involved. This principle was raised to the level of a national psychosis among decent people in Nazi Germany, and the monument to organized immobility of conscience may be found at Dachau near Munich.

One way to describe the jungle would be to call it a place of spectators, where most creatures are not even curious enough at the death struggle of another to raise their heads from feeding. But above the question of elementary order is the moral issue: to remain inactive at a moment of life-and-death decision is also to choose, to choose guilt. This is the basic reason why Christians, to the degree that they have something to report, cannot be silent. They must be "missionary-minded," they must be "evangelistic." And to the extent they have self-understanding, they will not deny to others the same right to attempt to persuade which they properly consider a dimension of their own liberty. It is valuable to the dialogue that Judaism should be "missionary," and that the reform movements of Buddhism, Hinduism, and Islam should be sending missionaries to the great cities of Europe and North America. Far better than the knife, far superior to ethnicity in religion, is open discussion of the things that matter most.

The rules of the dialogue are relatively simple: basically, to dialogue is to listen as well as to speak. It is to do so with the knowledge that we can learn from each other. Upon a foundation of basic concern for the other person, I have of course no obligation to agree with what he says unless it speaks to my condition. But I do have an obligation to hear what he says, and to be able to prove it by stating his position in a way acceptable to him. Even in the dialogue of classical antiquity it was recognized that discussion was foolishness (*amathia*) apart from the reference to ultimate truth. In the modern era, where the church meeting has contributed so fundamentally to the style of the various forms of town meeting, the ultimate reference is even more obvious. Dialogue is not mere conversation, a pointless passing of the time of day.

There are two principles to be observed if a meaningful discussion is to be held. The first is that each participant must have the stance of "good faith" in the dialogue. Confusion on this issue is the basic reason why, in laying the totalitarian ideologies to rest, we have made very little progress in fifty years—particularly, I think, among church and university people. In spite of all the concrete evidence to the contrary, our academic commitment to a speculative notion of freedom is such that we still define Communism and fascism as points of view, as sets of opinion. Yet they are not: they are conspiracies, instruments of subversion and espionage. They are not, and do not intend to be, enlightening to the public opinion.

They reject the whole process of dialogue and self-govern-ment as a "liberal fallacy." To be specific, convinced mem-bers of the Communist Party or the John Birch Society have no place in the dialogue: they have opted out of it; they do not believe in it (i.e., are not in "good faith" in the forum); and they would deny the liberty of it to others once they gained a position of power to so do. They demand a freedom for themselves which they are determined to deny to others. They should, therefore, be isolated and muted where possible, and jailed where overtly destructive.

The relationship of a convinced totalitarian to the dialogue is analogous to the relationship of a devout Christian Scien-tist to a medical school or a devout Hindu to a meat-inspec-tion station. (Fortunately, the Christian Scientist and the Hindu do not demand positions of decision which they cannot conscientiously fulfill. But Communists and fascists do, and there lies the problem.) If he is sincere, i.e., in "good faith," he will have nothing to do with such a post. He may make major contributions in some other role, but only the most speculative logic would call it unfair to deny such respon-sibilities to a person who cannot reasonably function in the assigned task.

It was more than disconcerting to see president, faculty senate, and student newspaper at the University of Illinois flunk their exams some months ago at this very point. In the name of "freedom," Professor Revilo Oliver was to be pro-tected from disciplinary consequences in his vicious and ob-scene attack upon the reputation of a dead man—John F. Kennedy. There is, of course, an interesting question of intel-lectual competence: e.g., just how long does a university con-sider itself bound in the name of an abstract "freedom" to finance an astronomer (with tenure) who has come to believe and proclaim that the moon is made of green cheese? Far more fundamental, however, is the objective fact of Oliver's membership at that time in the executive committee of a subversive organization—one which frankly and fully denies the theory and the practice of dialogue. The very foundation of the intellectual academy is responsible dialogue; what just claim has an individual who does not believe in dialogue, and refuses to live by its rules, to enjoy its benefits and securities?

Such a person may not have to be jailed, if no clear and present danger exists. He may be viable on the assembly line or in the forestry service, but he has no place in an institution whose very charter of existence is the encouragement of a raging dialogue, of full, free, and informed discussion. For the free society to exist, the free associations must maintain standards of discipline appropriate to their creative functions and responsibilities. A Christian congregation can hardly be condemned for disfellowshiping a vocal Buddhist, and a university worthy of the name will not tolerate a disciplined enemy of open-faced dialogue. None of us is under obligation to listen to those who broadcast at us from a soundproofed room: let them buzz in the isolation that they have created for themselves!

If the first principle of sound dialogue is restrictive, the second is more liberal. This derives from the question whether or not dialogue with the unbeliever is possible—a matter which Professor Hendrik Kraemer once discussed very fruitfully in *Wending*.[4] Certainly the most fruitful experience most of us have had with dialogue has been in small groups with whom we share a common destiny: chiefly co-believers or professional peers. Nevertheless, we moderns live in a shrinking world, one in which the opinions and concerns of persons in Berlin and Tel Aviv and Tokyo have a direct bearing on our lives. At the time my father was born, persons in St. Louis could live in relative oblivion of events in San Francisco or Boston. Today, what is happening in Jackson, Mississippi, may be determining whether your son and mine shall die in some stinking swamp in Borneo or Bangweulu, victims of the moral indifference of uncaring fathers, who have allowed a robbers' band of white primitives to hold power and to harass and brutalize a temporarily helpless section of the world's majority peoples.

On our American campuses we have now not only powerful communities of Catholics and Jews, as well as the major Protestant denominations, but also clubs of Hindus, Buddhists, Muslims. Where such exist, they too share in the discussion by which the university fulfills its function. Moreover, they represent a world issue of growing importance: the encounter of Christendom and most of the ancient centers of the faith. The official Christian attitude to other systems of being has been one of total rejection. The psychology of the Crusades has controlled our responses. The time is at hand, however, especially when their own reform movements are abandoning coercion and territorial definitions and entering the work of missions, to recover the genius of the "Logos Fathers" of the ancient Church. In the early period of Christian history, Christian interpreters were not afraid to welcome truth by whomever and wherever it was put forward. They courageously affirmed that He who was Truth Incarnate gathered up in His person and work all the truths put forward by all other teachers, and they were open to the dialogue with non-Christian schools of thought in a way that has been neglected until quite recently among the Christians.[5]

The developing Christian-Marxist dialogue, encouraged by Catholic officials since John XXIII and sponsored by ecumenical agencies such as the World Council of Churches and the National Council of Churches, belongs in this category. How can this be so, if individuals under totalitarian discipline have no place in the dialogue? The important fact is that in some European cultures, Marxism has become a world view, a "system of being" comparable to Christian culture-religion. In some metropolitan areas of France, Italy, and Germany, Marxist thought has had important cultural and educational centers for a century. There are families severed from Christianity and Marxist in belief for three and four generations. Just as Christian culture-religion has lost the apocalyptic drive and dynamic of early faith, so this Marxist culture-religion is very far from the all-or-nothing mood, discipline, and ethos of the professional revolutionaries. Where the participants are not under a secret discipline which prejudges and subverts the dialogue, where there is an honest intention to discuss in the context of ultimate truth, dialogue between the most disparate partners may well be useful although very difficult.

Not only need we have no anxiety at such encounters: we have every cause for rejoicing that our American pattern of religious liberty makes meaningful dialogue possible to a degree utterly impossible under any system of coercion. The participants who present questions and affirmations in enjoyment of religious liberty can appear without masks, with the open face of truth. This was literally impossible, or was at most limited to martyr spirits, in former times. One apocryphal tale may suffice to establish the point. The tale is told that during a visit of agents of the Holy Office (the Inquisition) to the University of Paris, during a "McCarthyite" spree in the high Middle Ages, one instructor was interrogated as to whether or not he professed the threefold God of the Holy Trinity. Rumor had accused him of heresy, and the rack was mentioned as a fit end. He is said to have replied that rather than be put on the rack he would if necessary profess a fourfold God!

With liberty respected and the rules of the dialogue observed, we have a fair chance that our partner in the discussion actually means what he says; and thus the spark of truth may be passed, unintimidated and undefiled, from man to man. The achievement of religious liberty was a historical one, one to which certain men and Christian movements contributed immeasurably, and it ennobles and defines a relationship between persons who are its beneficiaries, whether they today remember its presuppositions or not.

A SPECIFIC LIBERTY

In the Universal Declaration of Human Rights, adopted by the United Nations, article 18 reads as follows:

> Everyone has the right to freedom of thought, conscience and religion; this right includes freedom to change his religion or belief, and freedom, either alone or in community with others and in public or private, to manifest his religion or belief in teaching, practice, worship and observance.[6]

This statement is both more comprehensive than the provisions for religious liberty in the federal Constitution and at the same time far less significant. Most of the subscribing governments seem to view it as signatory powers viewed the Kellogg-Briand Pact of 1928, as a pious façade behind which the old crude and callous practices of sacral society can be carried on. Most significantly, only by extension is there any protection for evangelism and missions in the statement. Yet religious liberty is far from complete without the right to compete in a free forum for men's convictions. Without the exercise of that right, religion atrophies and declines to the level of a pigmy private piety. Religious liberty is not— historically or theologically—a mere negative to state power to protect individual idiosyncrasies.

While Communist, Muslim, conservative Buddhist, and Roman Catholic governments commonly restrict evangelistic work by other groups, their adherents are insistent that in areas of freedom they shall have unrestricted rights of propaganda. Most striking is the way in which Islam, Buddhism, and Hinduism have recently produced missionary movements—always, as in Christianity too, in the reform wings seeking renewal of the religions. For many centuries the other high religions, like Christendom, defined the encounter in terms of closed territories. Their perspective was tribal and ethnic or, later on, national. But now new societies and mosques and temples throughout Europe and North America indicate that in the age of popular movements all systems of being must learn to compete openly and industriously with alternative creeds.[7] This is a tremendous advance in the history of human liberty. The lover of liberty will regard "missions" and "evangelism" as welcome alternatives to the old static and ethnic harmonism of religion and state power.

In some intellectual circles, influenced perhaps by Hindu views of "tolerance" and the Hinduism of an ultimate parity of all creeds and confessions, it is questioned whether missions are compatible with true toleration. Toleration is in any case an attitude to persons, not to doctrines. But more important, if religious liberty is conceived as a historical achievement rather than as a speculative idea, it becomes clear that the alternative to persuasion and dialogue is never, for very long, indifference: the alternative to argument and persuasion has been, and still is, recourse to violence. To date, although there is a good deal of harmonism and pseudo-sophisticated religious indifference in the air, our courts have consistently declared freedom to propagandize an essential part of liberty, and our churches show no inclination to surrender that missionary work which is basic to their life commitment.

Nor should they: for acceptance of the responsibility to communicate is one of the fruits of love. Nor is the church's mission in conflict with the dialogue, although sometimes the baptized may forget the proper manner of proclamation and revert to the stance and the tone of voice of coercion. Rightly conceived and executed, religious liberty and the church's mission are coefficients of each other. Moreover, the Christian will welcome a universalism of perspective and claims when put forward by other systems of belief.

INTERRELIGIOUS DIALOGUE

Originally, the Free Churches went out from the sixteenth- and seventeenth-century state churches in criticism of their promiscuity of membership and their failure to maintain separation from the style of life in the society at large. Building upon a covenant, they introduced vigorous internal discipline. Membership standards were strict for full members, and probationary membership was commonly practiced. Mature Christians had to expect to swim against the stream and to be trained for survival in rough waters.

The major tragedy of the Baptists, the Methodists, and the Disciples/Christians, the most successful American revival churches, is that during the century of their triumphant mass evangelism and rapid growth they have virtually abandoned membership standards. Very little attempt is made to maintain theological, ethical, or moral discipline—either traditional or reworked—to arm the churches for spiritual warfare in the twentieth century. In many areas they have sunk, therefore, to the level of a flat and tasteless culture-religion. And a socially successful establishment may be as fatal to true religion as legal privilege. Only the moment of truth forced upon them by a violent racism may save the faithful from taking on protective coloration and disappearing into the background altogether.

In this situation, the former state churches which have continued the traditional standards in liturgy and worship, in catechetical or confirmation training, are frequently able to act with more vigor and integrity than historic Free Churches which have settled comfortably into social establishment. During the same period when the Free Churches of British background have been going to seed, a tremendous influx of Continental churches—chiefly Lutheran—shifted the statistical balance of American Protestantism. For a long time they remained outside the mainstream of American religious thought, primarily due to continuance of foreign language services and schools. This also served to keep intact in an ethnic way their sense of community identity and separation. But in the last generation they have entered the ecumenical scene with tremendous vigor and a sturdiness of liturgical and theological concern which has won them wide following and influence beyond their own ranks. The names of Sittler, Pelikan, Bratten, Marty, *et al.* signify a development unmatched in this generation by any of the older American Protestant churches of English background. Of the earlier tradition, only the Presbyterians seem to have retained an integrity and an impact of comparable significance.

Fortunately, we are in a time and place where the ecumenical dialogue is well developed at local as well as national and international levels, and where we can draw strength from each other. Lay people, who seldom follow denominational lines when they move from one city to another, perhaps have a natural wisdom superior to professional churchmen at this point. For there is not, to my knowledge, a single vital question now before American Protestantism which takes shape along denominational lines. The traditional parish or congregation is itself subject to the most serious questioning, and the chief movements of Christian action and witness are without exception interdenominational and ecumenical.

The Protestant-Catholic dialogue has also entered a new level of discourse. During the struggle with Nazism and Communism a kind of "concentration camp" fellowship had already developed among faithful minorities in Europe. But the real impulse came with the accession of Pope John XXIII, who in his short reign of four and one-half years succeeded in undoing much of the damage the Christian movement had suffered at the hands of the reactionary line which leads from Pius IX to Pius XII. In centers of dialogue like Temple University, the University of Iowa, the Ecumenical Institute in Dubuque, and the Notre Dame Colloquium, Protestants and Catholics are well on their way to a rediscovery and rearticulation of the common tradition of the Latin Church, before the Council of Trent (1545–63), Formula of Concord (1577) and Canons of the Synod of Dort (1618–19) terminated the sixteenth-century debates and fastened a semipermanent alienation upon a divided Christendom. American Christians, in spite of the disgraceful conduct of the Protestant underworld, but without the cruel heritage of the European wars of religion, have a peculiar opportunity for reconciliation and renewal. The questions now exercising Catholic leaders are precisely those once given primary attention by Protestants, and the Protestant-Catholic dialogue may serve to awaken again the children of the Reformation to our forgotten standards on use of the Bible, the importance of preaching, use of the vernacular (an intelligible idiom), the lay apostolate and the recovery of internal discipline and integrity.

The dialogue of Christians and Jews has become a basic part of the life of thinking Americans, ever since the National Conference of Christians and Jews began its work following the outbursts of religious bigotry in the 1928 election. This concern has become institutionalized in our major cities, and also on the most important public and state university campuses. Just ten years ago, after a decade and a half of cooperative work in the University Commission of the National Conference of Christians and Jews, the pioneer religious affairs centers at Cornell, Michigan, Ohio State, Minnesota, and Iowa moved ahead with others to establish the Association for the Coordination of University Religious Affairs (ACURA). In 1946 there were only two official centers of "dialogue on campus" in the United States. There are now coordinators or directors appointed by administrations to foster the dialogue on campus in schools from one end of the country to the other, and the old style of work—in which a liberal Protestant chaplain or student worker operated an established church, with a decent generosity toward "the others"—is passing from the scene. It is now stated with increasing boldness that a student is not equipped for his citizenship in the American World City unless he has a knowledge and understanding of the other major religious traditions besides his own.

The responsibility of Christians to God's First Israel is one of the major unresolved questions in theology and church history. In the first place, because of the normal overintensity of family quarrels, it was the one encounter with a non-Christian alternative which the Church Fathers badly handled. Stoicism, Platonism, Epicureanism, the mystery religions, the cult of the Great Mother, the religion of the astrologers—all were handled and defined with a high degree of success. But the definition of terms in relation to Judaism and the Jews was in most cases simply atrocious, and that failure was to have disastrous consequences when Christianity became a coercive establishment. The history of established Christianity, of Christendom, is a long and painful record of atrocities against the Jews—from the mob violence of the First Crusade through the forcible baptism of Spanish Jews under Ferdinand and Isabella; from the anti-Semitism of Martin Luther through the pogroms of "Holy Russia"; ending in our own time in the butchery of the Nazis and the indifference of the so-called civilized world to Dachau and Auschwitz and three dozen other camps dedicated to the "final solution" to the "Jewish problem." The question put to us has not yet been resolved, and it lies at the base of the high feelings aroused by Rolf Hochhuth's *The Deputy*: "Was Hitler alone guilty?"

Against those who long for an emancipated eternal gospel we have to learn to affirm the Jewishness of Christianity. Against the totalitarian mentalities and movements we must resolutely and readily confess: "We are spiritual Semites!" For the emergence of anti-Semitism is the earliest and easiest way to perceive when a supposedly Christian nation or people is going sour. For this reason the term "anti-Semitism" itself belongs to the earlier humanitarian approach to the problem: it is not race or culture but the Jewishness of our spiritual history which gives offense to the totalitarian mind-set. The reason is very simple, and it is theological rather than socio-logical: the Jew, whether he is personally a believer or not, is by his very existence a sign to the God of Abraham, Isaac, and Jacob. The Christians can apostatize. They can betray their baptism and become mere Gentiles again, as they were before God made them His own people. But the Jew can-not: he is hated by the heretics and by the ideologues not for his ideas or his cultic practices or his religion, but *simply because he exists.* Thus, particularly in the modern period of murderous totalitarian movements, when so many millions of the baptized have accommodated, have settled for a low-grade Canaanite religion (tribalistic rather than universal, racist rather than ecumenical, serving popular idols rather than bearing the incompatible witness), the destiny of the Old Israel and the New Israel is so intertwined that a new theology of the relationship is imperative. It can truly be said, and the insight is portentous, that those Jews who were slaughtered in Hitler's Europe died for what the Christians would have died for had they remained Christian.

From the Jews we learn, above all, the importance of the Law. Tottering on the edge of anarchy in many of our cities, with violent men securely lodged in many positions of power and decision, we need to be reminded that "righteousness exalteth a nation, but sin is a reproach to any people" (Prov. 14:34) and that "except the Lord build the house, they labor in vain that build it" (Ps. 127:1). If decent people cease to be aroused when the helpless and defenseless are set upon by dogs and other beasts, when the poor and deprived are denied due process of law, when the unlettered and unskilled are trapped into virtual serfdom, when lawless policemen brutal-ize those without an advocate, when justice and righteousness and mercy are made mockery by wicked men, this nation shall surely come under judgment—until the cities be destroyed and the land laid waste without inhabitant. When our Christian pulpits are accommodating and mute, and the preachers are deferential to the princes and powers of this world's darkness, the Jews are still there—a visible reminder that the Law is still teacher and judge. That, and precisely that, is the reason why not long ago the Jewish temple was bombed on Peachtree Street in Atlanta, why during debates on *apartheid* the white Afrikaaner tribesmen sitting on the back benches were calling out "Finkelstein, Finkelstein" in mockery of the three Jews still members of the parliament of the Union of South Africa, the three still trying to retrieve some slight measure of justice for the coloured and the blacks from a totalitarian government. The raging heathen know their enemies; the Christians should know better their brethren.

We Protestant Americans need our Catholic neighbors and our Jewish neighbors even more than they presently need us. Above all we need them because living with them can help us to bury forever the temptation to long for the good old days when we thought to have our way by force, and to develop instead by our voluntary discipline that quality of life and witness which can alone commend the evangelical faith in an age of dialogue.

▶ 5
THE NEW STYLE OF CORPORATE LIFE

VARIOUS writers have attempted to define the radical social change which confronts the churches, a change so vast that the cultural life of Americans a century ago was closer to that of the ancient Sumerians than to ours now. Some stress the "metropolis." Others, seeing the triumph of technics in industrial civilization, speak of the "technopolis." With an eye to the World City that America is becoming, the word "cosmopolis" or "oikupolis" may be most appropriate. In any case, the whole world—America as well as newer nations—has become an area of rapid social change. Any serious discussion of "long-range planning" must today plan for alternative routes and encountering the unexpected: new structures must be tooled for continual change rather than laid out in five-year or twenty-year plans. One of the major strengths of the open society, over against ideological systems, is precisely its flexibility.

On the other hand, certain major trends may be identified and discussed in relation to the effectiveness of Christian witness and service. Foremost in effect on many levels is the undeniable process of urbanization, which has both concentrated populations in metropolitan complexes and created an entirely new kind of countryside. According to a leading authority on metropolitan government, half of the American people now live in the twelve largest metropolitan complexes. Twenty-five per cent are concentrated in just 220 out of over 3,000 counties. Eighty per cent live within easy commuting distance of cities of at least 25,000 inhabitants.[1] Four out of 5 Americans have moved to another state since World War II, and 9 out of 10 live at least five hundred miles from their place of birth.

Within the lifetime of the older generation, so recently that Protestant imagery has not caught up with the change, the people of the United States have ceased to be a rural and agrarian folk and become city dwellers. Before the depression of 1893, 4 out of 5 Americans lived on farms or in rural villages. Of the 77,000 Baptist, 54,000 Methodist, 16,403 Lutheran, 13,200 Presbyterian, 7,784 Episcopalian, 7,769 Disciple, and 5,679 Congregational churches in 1950, 4 out of 5 were situated on the land. But the people were no longer there: they had moved to the city.

In terms of founding new churches, the denominations flourished during the last century and memberships generally increased more than the population. The Baptists quadrupled their congregations between 1860 and 1900, and added 27,000 congregations in the first half of the twentieth century. The Congregationalists more than doubled between 1860 and 1900, and then held steady for sixty years. Because of the difficulty in getting reliable reports from the Christian churches, the figures on the Disciples require interpretation: between

1860 and 1900 the number of congregations increased nearly five times; since 1906 the Disciples' congregations fell from 10,300 to 7,800 (1900 to 1950). Between 1860 and 1900 the Episcopal congregations more than quadrupled; there has been a measured increase subsequently. From 1860 to 1900 the number of Methodist congregations increased by 34,000; in both years they had the largest number of any denomination. During the twentieth century, however, the Methodists have barely held even, while the Baptists have forged far in the lead. From 1860 to 1900 the Presbyterians more than doubled the number of their congregations; in this century they have fallen from 15,500 to 13,200 congregations. During this same period the Catholics show the following increase: 1860—2,550; 1900—10,300; 1950—15,500.[2] Of all these churches only Lutherans and Catholics can attribute any of their considerable increases to immigration. Certainly worthy of reflection is the fact that the Congregationalists and the Methodists have just held even, while the Presbyterians have lost substantially. It would appear that the newer immigrations are more successful in meeting the challenge of the city than those English-language churches of older standing, even those of nineteenth-century revivalist expansion. Does this mean that the energies of these churches are being turned to the mastery of the problems of the Great City? Or does it only indicate a basic shift of the center of gravity in the American religious scene?

THE BACKWARDNESS OF PROTESTANT IMAGERY

The Protestant response to the problems of the Great City has not been a happy one. There is a recurring suspicion in Protestant circles that life in the city excludes the kind of human relations which might be called "Christian." It seems probable that this had deeper roots than American history, in which the earliest settlers became identified with the America of the agrarian period. Sectarian Protestantism, at least, has always had an affinity for the wilderness rather than the cities. Jerome's exclamation indicates how early the wilderness motif reasserted itself in the Christian movement, even though in its early decades the faith spread as a city movement through the synagogues of the diaspora:

O wilderness, bright with Christ's spring flowers!
O Solitude, whence comes those stones wherewith in the apocalypse the
    city of the mighty king is built!
O desert, rejoicing in God's familiar presence.
What are you doing in the world, brother, you who are more than the
    universe? [3]

Although the repeated effort to demonstrate that the Anabaptists and the seventeenth-century radical Puritans were organically related to medieval monasticism has proved fruitless, there is little doubt that these movements were often like monasticism in a certain cultural as well as spiritual austerity.

This may mean that American Protestantism, which owes so much to the "radical Reformation" rather than to the "magisterial Reformation," will have continual difficulty in coming to grips with a challenge such as that recently put by an authority on the city. According to John Osman of the Brookings Institution, himself trained in theology: "The logic of America is the city. . . . *Religion today is challenged to create an urban civilization.*" [4] If this be true, there is a pointed question to American Protestantism in Peter Berger's statement that "the concepts of community which our churches attempt to preserve in modern society are frequently agrarian concepts totally out of place in the urban situation." [5]

Truman Douglass, in an essay entitled "The Job the Protestants Shirk," cited the conclusion of the Amsterdam Assembly of the World Council of Churches (1948): "There are three great areas of our world which the churches have not really penetrated. They are: Hinduism, Islam, and the culture of modern cities," and challenged our own Protestant churches to abandon their romantic ruralism and meet the needs of the Great City.[6] The problem may be worldwide but, with the tremendous shift of population to the cities in America, it is especially acute here. The Protestant churches have only begun to experiment with ministries to the inner city. And even on the land the population uses radio and television, drives the same cars, wears the same clothes, eats the same breakfast food, i.e., lives in megalopolis. What we face is less an urban-rural split and more a new situation of complexity which pervades the whole social fabric.

The future of America lies with the Great City. Across the world map, the churches have failed thus far to penetrate the culture of cities. This kind of Protestantism has always shown an affinity to the wilderness rather than friendliness toward the accoutrements of civilization. In the course of American history, in establishment and during the great revivals, the center of gravity of the major Protestant churches was located in the countryside, and it is there yet. In this complex of circumstances, what chance is there that representative American churches will learn to minister to the men and women of the Great City? Is our faith, in short, effective only in societies where the village is the integrating social pattern?

If the program of most of our seminaries affords an answer, it must be in the affirmative: We are chained to the past. At a recent meeting of the American Association of Theological Schools in Toronto, Dean Walter Muelder of Boston University School of Theology said 80 per cent of our present seminary programs are obsolescent. The major reason is that they are geared to a situation that no longer exists. We are still training men to go out and give leadership in the "church on the green," to be a key voice of neighborly integration, to be active in friendly enterprises,

> . . . by slow prudence to make mild
> A rugged people, and thro' soft degrees
> Subdue them to the useful and the good.
> Alfred Lord Tennyson

When the young man goes out, however, he finds that he is only one in a Babel of voices of equal authority, that the members want to talk as well as listen, that the neighborhood (wrongly called "community") no longer exists as an entity, but has become a crossroads on the way to the city. What then shall he do? Shall he, as the last generalist in a specialized world, fight a rearguard action, participating energetically in those residual neighborhood efforts where a maximum of verbal facility and a minimum of specific information still qualify one for leadership: local politics, school activities, officiating at the "rites of passage" (those universal human experiences of birth, marriage, and death), not to forget the happy hunting ground of individual and family counseling? Or shall he retool his ministry and the equipment for it in terms of the new communities which do exist, where the people are hungry of spirit, where the dark jungles of an uncivilized world await the daybreak of redemption?

THE CALL TO SERVE

Our churches are not the only social institutions which have been tardy in making the institutional adjustments necessary to serve the people. One of the most scandalously retarded areas is legislative reapportionment in the states. Some states have for one and even two generations, and contrary to their own constitutional requirements, refused to provide just representation for the people of metropolitan areas. The city of Atlanta, Georgia, for example, with nearly one million population, can be neutralized in the legislature by two rural counties of 203,000 population. The uses of the county unit system, like the "rotten borough" system which obtained in Britain before the Great Reform Bill of 1832, are many; one of the foremost is to keep political machines in office which could never win an honest election. It is painful to record that Protestants, with their rural bias, have not seldom justified this wickedness rather than spoken up for justice and righteousness. At a recent hearing in New Hampshire a woman identified as a Sunday school teacher opposed reapportionment on the grounds that the rural and Protestant people were the backbone of America. If she had added "white" to her romantic primitivism, her argument could have been used in Georgia. Here again is an area where the U.S. Supreme Court (in the 1962 Tennessee Case) has had to give a moral leadership which our churches should long ago have initiated. Is it better patriotism to keep alive the great principle that the Founding Fathers enunciated, that "taxation without representation is tyranny," or to pretend that the political patterns which obtained among 3.8 million Americans at Jefferson's time (with a slave counting as three-fifths of a person) must be continued unchanged and unreformed among the present 200 million citizens?

But the church is called *to serve,* and where she neglects that apostolic commission it is far more serious than insensitivity or injustice at the political level. Eugen Gerstenmeier, founder of *Hilfswerk* in postwar Germany and now "Speaker of the House" (*Bundestagspräsident*) in Bonn, summed up our responsibility in this way:

> The church of Jesus Christ is a community of life based on faith and love. Therefore the church is to work together not only as a fellowship of knowledge (e.g. in its theology), or as a community of listeners active in liturgy (in common worship), but is above all to be dedicated to service, that is to firm action, for each other and for the need of the world.[7]

The temptation to flee into some new burst of intellectual discipline, or into some new expression of praise, is a real and very present one. As much as we need a renewal of theological and liturgical integrity in our churches, it is worth recalling that the New Testament lays much more weight on doing the Truth than on formulating it.

The scope of Christian service (*diakonia*) is broad. Hostile to the faith, both the Nazis and the Communists have demanded that the church "keep out of politics." The men of Barmen (May, 1934) answered that demand (with which even in the United States we are not familiar) with the second article of their Declaration, based on I Corinthians 1:30.

> Just as Jesus Christ is the pledge of the forgiveness of our sins, just so—and with the same earnestness—is he also God's mighty claim on our whole life; in him we encounter a joyous liberation from the godless claims of this world to a free and thankful service to his creatures.
> We repudiate the false teaching that there are areas of our life in which we belong not to Jesus Christ but another Lord, areas in which we do not need justification and sanctification through him.[8]

It is instructive to read the Nazi program for the Warthegau, a controlled area of resettlement in occupied Poland where they were able to carry through the narrow definition of the church which resistance prevented in the homeland.

4. There are no longer any relations to groups outside the district. . . .

7. Germans and Poles may no longer live together in one church. . . .

9. No special offerings may be collected above the annual dues.

10. The associations may own no property—such as buildings, houses, land, cemeteries—except for meeting rooms. . . .

12. The associations may not conduct social welfare programs which are alone and exclusively the affair of the NSV.

13. In the associations only native pastors from the Warthegau may be active.[9]

This was the church which the Nazis wanted: a private church, without missions, ecumenics, or service.

The Communist line toward the church is equally revealing. In East Germany, the attack is as follows:

1. The church must disappear from public view and be limited to purely church-cultic affairs. The claim of the church to be *Volkskirche,* that is church for the people, is strictly denied.

2. Above all, the church may not carry on any educational and youth work; social service is also denied her.[10]

Under both types of totalitarianism, the policy is to reduce the church to purely private religion. Dogmatic secularists and radical rightists make the same demand on the churches in America.

In the healthy society, by contrast, the church carries on imaginative and energetic witness to the Lordship of Jesus Christ over the whole world. The Atlantic City Conference on Christian Social Welfare (1957) pointed up two guidelines of special relevance to our discussion: the church is called "to provide experimental and demonstration projects based on evidence of emerging need in the community; to pioneer with a ministry in neglected areas." [11]

In a later chapter we shall discuss the usefulness of experiments and demonstrations by the churches. In the meantime, let us note: the Great City is the neglected image. What is the basis on which the churches can build new and redemptive patterns of service in the Great City?

THE NEW PRINCIPLE OF COMMUNITY

In *nomadic society* the basic principle of community was blood relationship, consanguinity. Land meant little or nothing, and the god of the people was jealous of localized shrines and hostile to agrarian fertility rites. In *agricultural society,* the village became the center of community. This is the pattern, originally defensive against raiders and marauders, with which our memory is filled. Here morality and ethics are primarily neighborly, grounded in geographical propinquity. In *industrial society,* a new principle of community is emerging, one not yet identified by the churches except in experimental situations.

The first studies of the society developing during the last century emphasized the depersonalization of human relations in the Great City. The term "anomie" was applied to the situation of the isolate, without "community," without *koinonia.* And in the early decades of the industrial revolution, the masses in the "labor supply" were often reduced to the status of things. Just as today in Johannesburg the laborers are detached from their earlier social identity without a new cohesion being given, so a century ago in Europe the people who flooded into the factory town were defenseless and fragmented, exploited, and abandoned by the churches. Men like Johann Hinrich Wichern and Frederick Denison Maurice warned in vain of the danger to church and state inherent in the atomism of the lonely crowd. Today, however, with the rise of social responsibility and the maturing of specialized functions in a complex society, new lines are appearing on the face of the city. These new and sophisticated communities are primarily professional and vocational rather than geographical, although there is of course a pronounced tendency for persons of like social status to reside in the same neighborhoods.

The key to integration in industrial society is no longer neighborhood, i.e., the city understood as a complex of villages. The key, which the Evangelical Academies and Lay Institutes have used to such good effect in postwar Europe, is the fact that the Great City is a highly complex network of professional and vocational communities. To the man of the village or countryside, when he first moves to the city, it seems as though no one knows anyone else: atomism, fragmentation, and anonymity seem dominant. And he may live out his life without ever thinking of the city as anything but a necessary evil, a place where one must live for the sake of a job. He may even demand of the church he joins that the hymns shall be the old songs, the preaching shall repeat the old phrases, the men's club shall artificially cultivate the first-name relationship with strangers—all of this is an atavistic effort to recapture the snows of yesteryear, when we were all boys together down on the farm! If he does this, he will condemn himself and his church to irrelevance and disservice.

In the Great City, however, the bankers know the bankers, the barbers know the barbers, the taxi drivers know the taxi drivers, the preachers know the preachers. The peer groups to which we belong, where our real conduct is shaped, are professional and vocational. This is the real cruelty of forced unemployment today: not that people starve, but that without a place in the world's work, without a functional peer group, a person is something less than a man. The automobile worker, although he probably does not even know the names of the people on the same floor in the apartment building or down the street in the city, feels a sense of identity with the man on the line in Montgomery, South Bend, and Arlington that will withstand all but the most extreme pressures. And is there any doubt as to the "we group" which controls the morals and ethics of the medical doctors? Is there any evidence that the churches or universities have any real influence on the conduct of those who are, or should be, the stewards of public health? Or is their conduct influenced almost exclusively by the union, the tightest closed shop in the country, the American Medical Association?

The reason why we have a "church language," which makes Sunday morning seem so utterly unrelated to the rest of the week—even the rest of the minister's week—is that we have largely failed to date in the job of interpreter. Reinold von Thadden-Trieglaff, head of the great layman's movement the *Kirchentag,* said once that the way churchmen handle laymen's questions is to restate them in terms of answers that the church has had for a long time, and then give back to the laymen answers to questions they never asked! Another way to say the same would be this: We take the laymen's questions, restate them in the language appropriate to the situation when we were all generalists in an agrarian culture, and give back answers which evoke a fond memory, and sound all right, but are in fact irrelevant. Many of our schools for the clergy are more or less openly dedicated to training "pulpiteers," and during the second period of American church history when the essential task was to "get it said" at least once, and compellingly, to as many people as possible, this was right. Today, however, what we need is clergy who can listen as well as speak. What we need are "interpreters."

The central building at the fine lay training center of the United Church of Canada in Paris, Ontario—Five Oaks Christian Centre—is called "The House of the Interpreter" (a phrase taken from the almost forgotten classic, *Pilgrim's Progress*). This is the minister's present assignment: to interpret the real questions of the people back into the world of the Bible, and to translate the Word into the day-by-day, on-the-job life of the *Laos,* the church in the world.

When our seminaries begin to retool to equip men and women for the interpreter's role, we shall begin to move out of our obsolescence into the encounter with the needs of the age. We must leave the protectionist stance, abandon the haste to build a continuing city. We must begin to take seriously the criticism of Dietrich Bonhoeffer: ". . . the church has fought for self-preservation as though it were an end in itself, and has thereby lost its chance to speak a word of reconciliation to mankind and the world at large." [12]

After all, Christ died for the world, not for the church!

THE APOSTOLATE OF THE LAITY

In the era of the Great City, in the third period of American church history, ministers need to master the art of listening as well as speaking. At the 1959 Conference of the European Directors' Association of Evangelical Academies and Lay Institutes, Eberhard Mueller of Bad Boll put the issue in a dramatic formulation. He said that he had been trained as a Lutheran theologian to believe the Word and the Sacraments to be the centers of Christian life, the two primary forces carrying the Christian movement. He now had come to feel that a third mark of the church must be added: dialogue (*Gespräch*). In the fullness of time, we had come to a point where laymen were no longer content to sit in silence and follow in docile obedience: they would be bound only by decisions which they had had a part in making. It is illuminating to note the way in which Dr. Mueller, a leading churchman of the Church of Württemberg, a land church, has come to a practical conclusion so like that expressed by our Free Church fathers, in terms of the restitution of the New Testament church: in the Free Church, decision is reached by discussion which leads to a consensus. Christian decision is not made by the magistrate; neither is it laid on the church by a hierarchy or a priestly class. It is reached under the guidance of the Holy Spirit in a meeting where all who share the common destiny participate.

To revive the apostolate of the laity, to take seriously the vocation of the whole people of God in the world, may mean the introduction of "new methods" as radical as the camp meeting and field preaching and public disputations were at the beginning of the Great Awakening. The preaching service itself may require restructuring, that the sermon again speak to the condition of the people, i.e., be "edifying" in the scriptural sense. Old leaders of the German Student Christian Movement have reported on the dramatic effect of the introduction of the "talk-back" session in the university congregation at Berlin before World War I. The chaplain (Traugott von Hahn) began the custom of passing out each Sunday small cards on which were given the topic and text for the following Sunday. Readings were given for the weekdays, with two or three questions for reflection in preparation for the coming sermon and service. After the service and the benediction, each week, the preacher stepped down from the pulpit to the center aisle, gathered the genuinely concerned, and answered questions, heard criticisms, finished the translation of the Word into the idiom of those questioning. Reinold von Thadden-Trieglaff has testified that, although he came from a pious and churchgoing home, it was in this situation that he first learned what the sermon was supposed to do. It was not just part of the program, which the people might watch with hands in pockets and compare with other performances—as they might today choose between Channel 5 and Channel 11. The sermon is to communicate, and the people share in the process of communication. If it does not communicate, then it is not the Word at all. The Word is not a cement block, with which interaction is impossible: the Word is on His way to become flesh in a living people.

The Evangelical Academies and Lay Institutes are not training centers to equip the laity "for work in the church": they exist to arm the laity for work in the world. This is a fundamental difference from most of the "Lay Academies" and "Christian Communities" which recently have sprung into existence in America. The American academies and communities are dedicated to training "lay theologians," and since "thinking Christianly" is in short supply among clergy and laity in American Protestantism, these programs are worthy of all good will and support. But there is an acute temptation not to take the "dialogue with the world" seriously, as can be seen for example in the effort of several graduate schools of religion to establish what amounts to a "Christian university within the secular university." Because we have not succeeded in communicating with the fine arts, the humanities, the social sciences, we establish within the divinity school a series of chairs in Religion and Art, the Church and Mass Media, Contemporary Literature and the

Christian Faith, Christianity and Race Relations, etc. By domesticating the encounter we remove its sting. The American centers which stress theological literacy, as useful as they can be, are in danger of avoiding the real ground of dialogue —the border area between the faith and a world come of age. To take the world seriously—that is the needed exercise, the necessary venture of faith!

The nearest thing to an Evangelical Academy in America is a good university extension program. There is a university on the Great Plains, for example, which cosponsors a series of intensive educational programs with the Visiting Nurses Association in the western part of the state. For each of the sessions, three or four experts in public health, social legislation, state government, or related subjects will be flown out to a county seat five hundred miles distant from the campus. Nurses will be gathered in from an area within a radius of seventy-five miles, and the lectures and discussion will deal with technical advances, wage legislation, professional standards; occasionally an issue involving professional ethics and morals will come up for consideration. This is precisely the kind of conference along vocational professional lines— with nurses, doctors, lawyers, elementary school teachers, postal employees, policemen, personnel managers, automobile workers, bakers, barbers, beauticians, dance instructors, shop foremen, etc.—which run constantly at Bad Boll, Tutzing, Loccum, Arnoldshain, Boldern, Kerk en Wereld, and the other European lay institutes. But there is one significant difference: the conferences in the European lay institutes always include the theological dimension, the issue of ultimate responsibility without which all discussion is foolishness. The problem of "the responsible society" is thus given its appropriate setting. There is no effort to mute the encounter: it is the job of the theologian to communicate, to speak in the language of the vocational and professional grouping involved. The interpreter's business is not to teach the language native to him, the "church language": it is to make the Word intelligible in the vernacular.

Each vocational and professional grouping has its own idiom, and the role of the interpreter is to learn to speak it. This means that in serving as a useful chaplain to the laymen in their ministry in the world the clergyman will have to specialize. As the last generalist in an increasingly specialized society, he is seemingly reduced to the statement of timeless truths and verities in universal human experiences. The general ministry is, however, that which all Christians share by virtue of the ordination of their baptism. In the New Testament, "the ministry" is the ministry of the whole church; when specifics are dealt with, "ministries" is the term used. The New Testament church is engaged, as it were, in a "group ministry." Yet how often a man engaged in the ministry to the campus, or to men in military service, or to persons in hospitals or prisons is greeted with the question: "When are you going back into the ministry?"

Here again we see the idea of a "normal" ministry raising its head, in which the clergy conduct monologues and "lead" the laity. In fact, there are many ministries. And the most exciting experiments in the ministry to the inner city[13] as well as in the countryside[14] involve a style of group ministry which allows for specialization. A city parish or group of churches with 90 doctors, 150 schoolteachers, 75 real estate men, 75 personnel managers, etc., can certainly support a chaplain for each vocational group in the joint ministry. And the development of a special ministry capable of hearing and understanding the real problems, tribulations, sins, and pos-

sibilities for good of the various stewardships will go hand in
hand with the awakening of a general ministry of the laity.
At present they are frustrated because the laymen feel that
the minister does not really understand their situations, and
the clergyman feels that the laity are indifferent to what he
preaches. The real problem is that the concern of the Reformation has not been met: the Word has not been translated
into the vernacular.

There is another live concern of the sixteenth-century Reformers involved in the work of the Evangelical Academies
and Lay Institutes: work which is performed in the fear of
God and love of one's fellows is conceived as a "vocation"
(*Beruf*) and not as a "job." For Luther, and in this he was
followed by Calvin and others, a vocation performed in good
conscience toward God and man was a religious office, and
the one performing it was as truly one of "the religious" as
if he were a clergyman or a professor of theology. The "priesthood of all believers" meant not only that each Christian is
responsible before God for his fellows, but that in the stewardship of his vocation or calling he was responsible before
God for his life and work in the world.

The primary work of the European lay institutes has been
in the rehabilitation of vocational and professional communities, in the creation of stewardships where a few years before
the law of the jungle had ruled. They have had an important
role in proclaiming the significance of dialogue and in training numbers of people in discussion methods and work
with small groups. They have also taken the lead in preparation of study units and monographs, and in holding conferences on themes which in America are normally sponsored
by boards and agencies: "Christianity and World Peace,"
"The Churches and Racism," "Christians and the Respon-

sible Society," "The Churches' Contribution toward European Union," etc. But the really dramatic development, the type of work which makes a historical breakthrough in the evangelization of social structures, is the development of ways of relating the gospel to the new communities which line the face of the Great City.[15] In doing this, they have made the living word what it is meant to be: "The human speech heard by specific men at specific times in a specific situation, in a specific language and with a specific intention."[16]

The laity are not only so situated as to be in effect the cutting edge of the church in the world; they are also unable to fall easily into some of the superficial moralisms with which the clergy, protected and "paid to be good," on occasion satisfy themselves. It is the dialogue of the church with the world which, if taken seriously, can bring Jesus Christ back from the borderline to the center of real life.

THE LESSON OF THE CHURCH STRUGGLE

The failure to complete the translation of the Word leads in our time to wholesale apostasy on the part of the baptized. That is the lesson to be learned from the church struggle. The completion of the translation, the formation of a community of faithful people, is not a desirable new church program to replace the Sunday School movement, so to speak, now that the latter has peaked and begun to decline. Lay training, lay initiative—these are the present paths to faithful witness is speaking and acting. A church which has shunned the frontier, the borderline of church and world, to dwell within a self-contained fortress or to identify uncritically with the prevailing culture, will lose both liberty and truth.

In 1934, when the collaborators with Nazism were making

their drive to capture the church offices of the Old Prussian Union (*APU*), Martin Niemoeller and Dietrich Bonhoeffer sent out over their signatures a warning to the baptized. Niemoeller, former U-Boat captain and popular suburban preacher, was soon to begin eight and one-half years of incarceration as an object of Hitler's personal animosity. Bonhoeffer, leader in the German Student Christian Movement and in the World Alliance for International Friendship through the Churches, was to be martyred for his part in the July 20, 1944, plot on the dictator's life. The statement warned against the danger of "apostasy." In doing so it raised—as did Bonhoeffer's development of the doctrine of "heresy" in his ecumenical theology—an issue long buried in the easygoing culture-religion of official Germany.

Not just the common folk, but even professional theologians and church historians had assumed an identity of German *Volk* and church, a consonance of German cultural values and civilization with Christian principles. The Christian German nation was presumed to have inherited the mantle of the Holy Roman Empire. When the last Kaiser declared war in 1914, he called the loyal sons and daughters of the German Reformation to a holy crusade against the schismatic Orthodox of Russia and the unreformed Catholics of France. Far into the years of the Weimar Republic, hundreds of German Protestant churches held annual special services on the occasion of the exiled Christian Emperor's birthday.

In all this there was implicit a creeping corruption, an unfaithfulness to the Lord of all history and all peoples, which went almost without challenge at first. Not until the party of the German Christians (*Deutsche Christen*) came to demand frankly that the church should serve as a pillar of the state and that there should be deleted from Christian teaching anything offensive to the sensibilities of the German race did some resistance arise. At this point the face of the "Anti-Christ," as Bonhoeffer referred to the claims of Nazism, became unmistakable and a minority of the baptized got the point.

At Fanö, Denmark (1934), Bonhoeffer attempted to get the ecumenical fellowship to adopt a statement which would clarify the issue of heresy vs. living orthodoxy. This failing, his own position was forthright: "He who severs himself from the Confessional Church severs himself from the grace of God." [17]

The raising of the issue of apostasy was indeed timely, even though the Confessing Church was popularly condemned for "intolerance" and "dogmatism," for the tragedy lay more in the apostasy of millions of baptized Christians than in the persecution of those who remained faithful. Persecution is an old problem for the Christians, and they have learned through the centuries what to do in the face of it. Nor should we forget that the twentieth century, this age of "the City of Man in the World of Tomorrow," is the bloodiest age of persecution that the church has lived through. More Christians live today under the sign of the fish, the ancient recognition symbol of the persecuted, than ever before. And larger sections of Christendom have been forcibly torn from the body of believers than in any time past, at least since the ancient centers of the faith in North Africa were overrun by Islam over a millennium ago. Yet persecution is not the scandal of the century: the scandal is apostasy. And it was the men of the Confessing Church who put their finger on the nature of the crisis, and in addition rejuvenated at Barmen (May, 1934) the forgotten practice of Christian confession of faith. Barmen, on which Professor Arthur Cochrane of Dubuque has published a major theological-historical study, was the most important confession in many generations of church history.[18]

In the Six Articles of Barmen, like all truly great confessions written "on the battlefront" rather than in an armchair, the major Christian convictions threatened by the totalitarian creed of Nazism were affirmed. And the assembly of delegates, composing the first united confessional assembly of Reformed and Lutheran churchmen since the Reformation, went on to damn the false teachings which were leading a baptized nation into wholesale apostasy. (Interestingly enough, in view of what men have learned of the nature of true tolerance since the sixteenth century, they condemned the errors but not the persons.) Niemoeller and Bonhoeffer were but drawing the necessary conclusions from the fact of Barmen when they warned against the perils of apostasy in their letter.

"Witness," as Barmen defined it and the Confessing Church affirmed it, was more than an intellectual confession of faith. *Bekenntnis* carries the double meaning of "confession" and "witness." In a similar sense, "apostasy" involves both lack of intellectual discipline and perversion of life. This joint relationship was written large during the Third Reich, and the resisting church never forgot the lesson. How could it happen that a "Christian nation," with long and proud generations of "Christendom" behind it, could prove unfaithful in confession and witness? This was the central problem of the Confessing Church, the problem faced at Barmen and dealt with in another way in the Stuttgart Declaration of Guilt (October, 1945). This is the besetting problem of Christianity in the twentieth century.

In the face of totalitarian Nazism and Communism, with all the terror and torment they have brought in the way of outside pressures, the basic problem of the Christian churches remains that of apostasy. The damage done by internal disloyalty and subversion is far greater than the damage brought by persecution, even today. There is more to be feared in the United States, for that matter, from self-styled champions of "militant Christianity" who attack the churches and the Christian colleges and seminaries, than there is from articulated atheism or Communism in our society. And of the countries which have gone totalitarian, it must be said with all possible accent:

—but for the faithlessness of the church of Russia, the reproach of Communism had never lain on Christendom;

—but for the faithlessness of the churches of Germany, the reproach of Nazism had never lain on Christendom.

This is the judgment which informs current discourse in Continental Protestantism, the sense of tragedy which makes it so difficult for well-fed and optimistic Americans to come to grips with the issues our partners in the "trans-Atlantic dialogue" are raising. With their peculiar combination of muscular religion and "spirituality," our churches are much closer to the style of pre-Hitler German Protestantism than they are as yet to mastering the lessons for all Christians which are to be read in the encounter with totalitarianism.

If we are to understand the nature of the great laymen's movements we must learn to appreciate what the church struggle signifies. For the *Kirchentag* (the "Rally of the Church") and the Evangelical and Lay Institutes are no mere organizational triumph. They represent an agonizing spiritual pilgrimage out of apostasy to rebirth, out of the lassitude of unbelief into the miracle of new Christian initiative rising out of the ashes. They signalize the rebirth of the church through movements of lay renewal.

Movements such as the *Kirchentag* and the *Akademien* cannot be taken over wholesale in any land, but both have proved to have more value as "exportware" than might have been thought at one time. Both now have fraternal movements, inspired by them and in turn developing new methods of lay witness, from Scotland to Japan to Indonesia.

THE RALLY OF THE CHURCH

With its impressive numbers, the *Kirchentag* has been the wonder and the despair of the rest of Christendom. In spite of attacks by Communists and neutralists in 1961,[19] the great rally still brought 110,000 persons to a mass demonstration in Berlin. And just before the wall was built, 13,000 came through "black" from the DDR (East Germany) to participate. In its most momentous public celebration (Leipzig, 1954), 675,000 rallied to the Crusaders' Cross of St. John.

For some time after the movement started, it was assumed that nothing comparable could be developed in other countries. So much of the appeal seemed to be essentially political —the natural response of a forcibly divided people to a great symbol of spiritual unity. And the great numbers—ranging regularly from one-fourth to one-third of a million—seemed so disturbingly Teutonic! Yet there were, as the rally gained international significance, fraternal developments in other countries. The Dutch responded first with *De Grote Trek,* a study program in preparation for participation in the *Kirchentag*—reinforced by smaller mass meetings held locally and (simultaneously) on a district basis. In 1955 French Protestants launched *Le Rassemblement Protestant,* and on a weekend in mid-October, 1956, some 55,000 united in a demonstration in Strassbourg. More remarkable yet, an eight-day *Kirchentag* with over 100,000 in attendance was held (after Frankfurt, 1956), in Indonesia among the Batak Christians. In 1957 a committee of friends of the *Kirchentag* in Scotland joined with those who had sponsored the Billy Graham Crusade in that land to found *Kirk Week*. *Kirk Week* brings together delegates from local parishes of the Church of Scotland—there are some 2,200 in all—and includes as well the concerns of the free churches. (The Church of Scotland is a free church today, but it is also the church of the land—two facts which seem contradictory only to those who have studied logic but not Scottish church affairs!) More recently there are *Kirchentag* affiliates working in Basel, Zürich, and Norway; and in the United States a remarkable development has occurred under the leadership of Dr. Loren E. Halvorson in "The Minnesota Project." [20] And in February, 1967, an area-wide approach was made to southeast Iowa under the theme "Direction: Southeast Iowa."

But the main question for us in America is not whether we, too, can bring the same tribute of numbers to Christian concerns that we regularly pay to football, political rallies, state fairs, and other interests which lie close to our hearts. The emphasis on numbers can be deceptive, and the essential genius of the *Kirchentag* can easily be misunderstood if chief attention is devoted to that aspect of the movement. How then shall we conceive of it if not statistically? Is there something in our experience to which we can relate the experiment so often dismissed, with wondering admiration, as impossible of duplication or adaptation in the American setting? There is. The *Kirchentag* is in fact like nothing so much as a great "Religious Emphasis Week" in which the target is a metropolis rather than a university campus.

The style of the *Kirchentag* is what might be called "satura-

tion evangelism." Like the cities under the hammerings of
all-out bombing attack toward the end of World War II, the
metropolis where a *Kirchentag* is held is penetrated in every
section of its life. The variety and richness of the programs,
by virtue of which everybody can do something for the common faith and there is something in the week for everyone,
is astonishing. If attention is concentrated solely on the vast
numbers, it is easy to confuse a *Kirchentag* with some skill-
fully promoted demonstration. The *Kirchentag* represents a
new type of evangelism, in which simultaneous translation is
going on along all the "wavelengths," in all the idioms, of
the Great City.

"Evangelism" is often too narrowly confined and stereo-
typed, and hence that term may lead to misunderstanding—
as though the limits of its effectiveness were set by the range
of the human voice rather than by the power of the Spirit.
The problem is that evangelistic thought and method in
America have tended to settle in fixation on the style of the
camp meeting and popular "pulpiteer," as though proclaiming the Lordship of Jesus Christ were an atavism. The great
"Rally of the Church" has moved ahead, maintaining vigorous streetcorner preaching, preaching in great assemblies,
house-to-house evangelism, and at the same time making use
of the most sophisticated modern techniques for breaking
up the hard and caked earth which soundproofs modern civilization against the Word of God. The three marks of the new
style of evangelism are these: (1) dialogue, (2) lay initiative,
(3) variety of programs ("shot-gun" approach).

Before the development of "town meetings" under the
Minnesota Project (1963–67), a well-run "Religious Emphasis
Week" on a great college or university campus was the near-
est thing to a *Kirchentag* in America. When adequately pre-

pared and properly run, such a week of concentrated effort is long on planning and comprehensive in impact. Chaplains, student leaders, and faculty spend months in preparation— in prayer groups, study and discussion, administrative and financial undergirding. In the week when the entire campus community is to be saturated, every valid agency is called into play: classroom, chapel, radio and television campus programs (where they exist), dormitory discussions, preaching in assembly, plays and movies, discussion groups, and personal counseling. Of course, there has been some comment in the last two or three years which would indicate that this particular technique for penetrating the life of the campus is losing ground. It can be said with some assurance that its effectiveness is almost always in direct ratio to the amount of careful planning, of genuine and dedicated effort, that has gone into the matter. At its best, such a week is tremendously worthwhile.

The same is true of the *Kirchentag,* for the great mass meetings which close such an event are but the gathering together of all the multitude of voluntary groups which have carried through before and during the week, and attracted to them the most varied and colorful spontaneous responses from the public at large. The 100,000 at the first major rally (Essen, 1950) and at the besieged Berlin rally in 1961; the 250,000 who came to Berlin in 1951, Stuttgart in 1952; Dortmund in 1963, Hannover in 1967; the one-third million at Hamburg in 1953, Frankfurt in 1956, Munich in 1959, Köln in 1965, came at the culmination of a huge variety of programs during the preceding week. Even the phenomenal turnout on the Rosenthal Meadow in Leipzig in 1954 (675,000), with its inescapable overtones of political protest, was in the end a product of months of preparatory study, commission work, and a solid week of streetcar evangelism, youth encampment, world church festival, and impressive group discussions all through the city.

Moreover, preparation is as varied and exacting as is the carrying through. The *Kirchentag* has, since 1955, a number of major permanent commissions cosponsored with the Evangelical Academies and the church organizations for men's work, women's work, youth work, and the student movement. These commissions are comparable to the boards and agencies of our American denominations (the Evangelical Church in Germany has no such structure, itself) and they circulate study units, general discussion materials, and even books in certain fundamental areas.

The Commission on the State of the Church works, as it were, under the rubric, "the judgment is begun, and first in the House of God" (I Pet. 4:17). Since Frankfurt, 1956, the meaning and use of private confession has been dealt with thoroughly, and the church of Hannover has officially reintroduced the practice.

The Commission on Family Life has been led by persons active in the Family Life Movement so prominent in European countries among both Catholics and Protestants. Just two years ago a new structure of law governing family life was enacted in the Federal Republic, prepared and fought through in good part by persons active in the *Kirchentag*. Moreover, the parental responsibility for the education of the children—affirmed in an excellent article in the Bonn Constitution—has led to a new and creative relation between family, church, and school system. Finally, since the life of the Christian family is most directly threatened by Communist totalitarianism in East Germany, the *Kirchentag*'s work in this area has proved a true rallying center for Christian parents in the current church struggle.

The Commission on Political Affairs has carried further the line of the Barmen Declaration:

> We repudiate the false teaching that the church can turn over the form of her message and ordinances at will or according to some dominant ideological and political convictions.
>
> We repudiate the false teaching that the state can and should expand beyond its special responsibility to become the single and total order of human life, and also thereby fulfill the commission of the church.
>
> We repudiate the false teaching that the church can and should expand beyond its special responsibility to take on the characteristics, functions and dignities of the state, and thereby become itself an organ of the state.[21]

In this, the leaders of the rally have attempted to act responsibly in "Germany's second chance at democracy"; in the process they have come under savage attack from the new totalitarianism, too—both Communist and Neo-Nazi.

The Commission on Economic Justice, the Commission on Rural and Village Life, and the Commission on the Church in Industrial Society complete the roster. In 1954 a Commission on Ecumenical Affairs was founded because regularly several hundred representatives from sister churches abroad arrived to participate; at Frankfurt, 1950, indeed, the number ran to 1,600 and at Berlin, 1961—in spite of heavy dependence on air travel—to 1,300. In 1961 an outstanding event was the work of a new Commission on Christian-Jewish Relations.

Each rally functions under a special slogan (*Losung*), with major events linked to it thematically. These linking themes have been as follows:

Hannover, 1949—"The Church in Motion"
Essen, 1950—"Save the Human Being!"
Berlin, 1951—"Nevertheless, We Are Brethren!"
Stuttgart, 1952—"Therefore Choose Life!"

Hamburg, 1953—"Throw Not Away Your Trust!"

Leipzig, 1954—"Be Joyous in Hope!" (This theme was linked to that of the Evanston Assembly of the World Council of Churches—"Jesus Christ, the Hope of the World!")

Frankfurt, 1956—"Be Ye Reconciled with God!"

Munich, 1959—"Thou Shalt Be My People!"

Berlin, 1961—"Lo I Am with You!"

Dortmund, 1963—"Living with Conflicts"

Köln, 1965—"Stand Fast in Liberty!"

Hannover, 1967—"Blessed Are the Peacemakers!"

Although an over-all pattern of consistency is sought, a courage almost reckless is shown in encouraging dozens of lay voluntary groups to prepare their own special programs for showing during the week of "saturation evangelism." The total program of the *Kirchentag* is a book of no modest proportions, and the following are some of the "wavelengths" used:

1. Special services, including those in foreign languages and other liturgies, in all churches in the area.

2. Streetcorner preaching.

3. House-to-house visitation teams.

4. Preaching services in police precinct stations, in homes for the aged, in jails, prisons, hospitals, etc.

5. Prayer breakfasts.

6. Special luncheons for topical speeches and discussions.

7. Youth encampment and services.

8. Children's services.

9. Musical concerts: orchestral, choral, chamber music groups, opera, operetta, vocalists.

10. Plays, both classical and modern.

11. Art exhibits: architectural design, sculpture, water-color, oil painting, photography.

12. Topical lectures to thousands, held simultaneously in large auditoriums in the city.

13. Topical panels and forums, with written questions sent forward from audiences of tens of thousands, in great halls at the fair grounds.

14. Special journalistic inserts on "News of the Christian World," featuring articles and reports from the mission field, from experimental ministries to countryside and city, in the daily newspapers sold on the streetcorner.

15. Hundreds of small-group discussions on sensitive themes, scattered in homes and committee rooms throughout the city.

16. Radio and television broadcasts of key events and special programs, such as interviews with leading churchmen from abroad and from the Younger Churches, throughout the week.

17. Book reviews and exhibits by publishers, authors, and critics.

18. Pageants, parades, and window displays.

19. Large meetings relating the gospel to vocational and professional groups, with the discussants from among national and international leaders.

20. Panel discussions on major public issues, with state and national political leaders of Christian conviction.

21. "Old home day" rallies, based on the states from which newcomers to the area have recently come.

22. Good movies in all moviehouses during the week, with panel discussions of their "messages" and aesthetic merit.

The list is extended as various volunteer groups or service clubs with imagination and daring think of a new idiom and a new wavelength where they have something to say.

No channel is left unexplored by means of which some sector of the population may be reached. There is something for everyone, however simple, however sophisticated. The communication is verbal, visual, or indirect; the channels range from person-to-person encounter to existentialist lectures, and modern art and theater programs.

All that is needed, basically, is a common agreement in time schedule as to the days when dozens of voluntary groups will center down on the concerns of a single metropolis. There seems no real reason, except for our limited perspectives on evangelism, why any major metropolitan area of the United States could not benefit by this "saturation" approach.

MORAL COURAGE

The *Kirchentag* stands in legitimate succession to the awakenings of religion in the nineteenth century in Germany and Scandinavia, and fraternally to the great revivals of the same period on the North American continent. It is no more radical in its day than the field preaching and the camp meeting when these "new methods" were first used.

The new movements of lay witness are not only characterized by joy and imagination, but by sheer moral courage. The story of the struggle with totalitarian Communism has been told, as well as some of the work of *Kirchentag* and Evangelical Academies in it.[22] An equal courage is shown in treating questions of righteousness and justice in the affluent society, and this can be just as difficult.

Just one illustration—the way the *Kirchentag* responded to the agonizing issue of the Eichmann trial. The trial ran during the Berlin, 1961, event. At a time when most of the journalistic and political leaders were simply silent, for lack of anything to say, the great rally planned one of the major discussions on "The Christian Responsibility to Israel." This was the session that the youth and students flooded, so that

28,000 persons pressed into the great hall to hear this fateful question treated. The *Kirchentag* invited the chief rabbi of the *Bundesrepublik* to make the opening address. And in the preparatory literature which went out to thousands of parishes for study in advance of the rally, one section was devoted to questions on the Christian responsibility for the Jews; under it were pictures of the looting of the synagogues on the "Crystal Night," of the bodies stacked at Dachau, and one of Hitler standing in the rubble outside his bunker, with the subtitle *War er allein schuld?* ("Was he alone guilty?"). Only he who draws the knife shall win Isaac! We shall not see great evangelism in America again until we have foresworn shortcuts, cast aside "cheap grace," and recalled that the Baptism of Repentance always precedes the Baptism of the Spirit.

THE AMERICAN METROPOLIS

When the translation of the Word lags, or no living Word touches the real life of the modern society, whole populations are distraught and destroyed. In this day of anti-Christian ideologies, the peoples once Christian do not stay unformed and unimpassioned: they go bad. This is the lesson of the church struggle in the Third Reich, in the Communist areas, and in a growing number of American cities.

Effective translation, in word and action, can no longer be accomplished by professional churchmen. It takes place among laymen intent on renewal, among men of good will participating in the life of dialogue, in the midst of the world's work. Culture-religion descends—under pressure or temptation—into open apostasy. The church turned inward, sectarian and fortress-minded, ends in fossilized irrelevance.

The task is to span the bow more tautly, to build up a true church for a real world. To this end, there is a great need for models of lay discipline and covenant within the Christian movement; and for far greater openness to the secular order and respect for the issues and decisions of real life than the masses of the church people have previously shown. The solution is not to close rural chapels and open inner city cathedrals, although the displacement of Protestant churches from the people has serious consequences in fixing a mind-set of romantic ruralism in Protestant culture. The solution lies, in this moment of history, in the realization that the complex industrial society is not productive of anonymity and loss of personality at all—unless those who live in it fail to master the style of life and commitment which the new pattern of community based on profession and vocation and socioeconomic role entails. The effectiveness of the churches today will be determined by the speed with which they can shift from the generalities of an earlier social and economic order to the realities of a complex and highly sophisticated order. This shift must be accomplished largely by the laity.

► 6

THE SECULAR
CITY AND
CHRISTIAN
SELF-RESTRAINT

IN 1967, Father Hesburgh, C.S.C., president of
Notre Dame, called together some six hundred American and
European theologians to discuss the follow-up to the Ecumenical Council, Vatican II. The level of discourse is indicated by the participation of Fathers Gottfried Diekmann,
Bernard Häring, Yves Congar; Dr. Robert McAfee Brown;
Rabbi Abraham J. Heschel, *et al.* In the course of a week of
intensive work the question was asked: "What work must be
done before Vatican III?" After considerable excitement the
consensus seemed to be this: The area most acutely requiring
attention is the development of a *Theology of the Created
Order.* Being interpreted, we need a theology for the area
where lay people spend most of their time—in the midst of
the world's work. Or, to put it another way, the theologians
need to develop in the language of their own craft some

comprehension of the structures and relationships which the vast numbers of church members simply take for granted. We were accustomed to assume that "training the laity" meant bringing the unordained to seminars where they can learn to talk the church language. The painful thought is now arising that when "training the laity" is really taken seriously, at least half of the effort must be put forward by those whom Father Congar once called "the other laity," i.e., the clergy. They must learn to move out of the securities of the archaic and familiar, abandon the linguistic "strategy of terror" by which the masses have traditionally been kept under control, and begin to talk in the vernaculars of the world's work. For there are other integrities and other liberties besides those of the church, and we do wrong to suppose that important institutions in the world have value only to the extent they submit to church control, serve churchly interests, or at least explain themselves in churchly language. In a world come of age, theologians are beginning to remember—and sometimes to be forcefully reminded—that when the Creator gave dignity and liberty to His creatures, He included such creatures as Government (*Obrigkeit*), the City (*Polis*), and the University (*universitas magistrorum ac scholarium*).

THE TERM "SECULAR"

But, the style of doubt and denial persist. Creation and the secular are still viewed with suspicion among many of the pious.

Take a typical illustration of the misuse of the term "secular," which stems from a faulty understanding of the relationship of the "spiritual" and the "secular." A recent position paper adopted unanimously by the leadership of one of the great lay movements of the century starts out as follows:

All groups that bear the name of Christian are being challenged to-day as perhaps never before since the days of the Early Church. In the Western world, churches and Christian Associations no longer hold the position and influence which they once enjoyed. . . . Ours is a pre-dominantly secular climate, encouraging an outlook on life which for all practical purposes gets along without God.[1]

I would submit that this introduction moves in precisely the wrong direction. Historically, there is no evidence that the churches have lost prestige and influence, except in the sense that established religion has fallen into disfavor. There are those Christians, even in Communist lands, who believe that the present time of testing has been met by renewal movements and invigorated Christian witness. Most marked is the pejorative use of the term "secular" in the statement. Precisely at the time when both Catholic and Protestant theologians are saluting the laity as the bridge into the world, the specter of the "secular" is raised in the negative sense. "Secular" is the key word, and the view is one of hostility rather than respect for the integrity of the created order.

Let me refer to a statement on the "secular" in a recent book by one of our abler Protestant theologians:

Any discussion of the relation of the church to culture in our age must be set against the massive backdrop of the contemporary absence of God. The church now lives in a society for which God is elusive, if not quite unknown, and the categories of the holy and the transcendent are apparently meaningless, empty, and useless. And surely the deep religious problems of the church . . . are caused in large part by the fact that this secular spirit has penetrated into the mind and heart of the church as well as penetrating the world outside it.[2]

In this statement, the "absence of God"—a profoundly compelling concept, if taken seriously—is somehow identified with loss of "the categories of the holy and the transcendent." But "holy" is not a category at all, biblically speaking: it is a quality of life. Some contemporary seers say (and not the most "secular," surely) that "transcendent" is no longer a useful way of speaking of the One who is *gegenüber,* the one who is encountered. Worst of all, from an Evangelical standpoint, where did the notion arise that the penetration of the church by a "secular spirit" is something new—let alone the penetration of "the world outside it"? What "world" is this— the "Christendom" of Trent and the Synod of Dort? What "church" is this—the monolith of Lateran Council IV? The whole historical and theological perspective is perverse.

How then is "secular" to be understood? Since Rufus Jones raised the issue at the Jerusalem Conference in 1928, "secularism" and "secular" have been pejorative terms in many theological circles. Even among Lutherans, with the great tradition of the orders of creation (*Schöpfungsordnungen*), latter-day pietism has led to a nonbiblical rejection of creation. Even among Catholics, with the majestic tradition of the Natural Law, the ghetto life of past generations in predominantly Protestant America has often led to a rejection of the public life. And among Protestants of the more radical type—of the Anabaptist/radical Puritan/Free Church line— there has always been a tendency to slide off into a Manichaean hostility of light and dark, fortress and field, church and world.

Yet the tide is turning, and a new breed of theologians assures us that there are creative and redemptive signs outside the church. We are advised not only to throw open the windows but to exit the fortress and join with others who would build the beautiful and just City of Brotherhood.

TOWARD A THEOLOGY OF THE CREATED ORDER

The two most lively theologians of creation in recent generations have been the Jesuit anthropologist, Teilhard de Chardin, and the ecumenical leader and martyr to Nazism, Dietrich Bonhoeffer. Both of these men were working in an area largely neglected, an area profoundly affected by man's expanded knowledge of the natural world. Driven by a sense of the need for new and comprehensive thinking—to escape the heretical repudiation of the world of nature into which sectarian groups were falling, to redeem the churches from antirevolutionary identification with colonial and imperial structures (i.e., rejection of the whole modern age of women's rights, popular suffrage, general education), to make sense of the vast time and space opened up by archaeology and astronomy (so fatal to a primitive religious cosmology)—both Teilhard and Bonhoeffer created new words and concepts. With very few guidelines to depend upon in contemporary religious thought they both skirted the very edge of heresy, as is inevitable with creative spirits charting new paths. Both of them, in their excitement, were carried away into the poetic license which in theology we call "ecstatic utterance." But their concern was sound and their thought must be sifted, not condemned.

The truth is that the function of the church itself cannot be understood, even in the church language, apart from the doctrine of the created order and God's purpose in and for it. The lay apostolate, according to *Lumen Gentium* ("The Dogmatic Constitution on the Church," from Vatican II), "a participation in the saving mission of the church itself" cannot properly be defined purely as an extension of churchly purposes. The lay apostolate stands on the frontier of "church" and "world"; its business is the dialogue of church and world; its style is one of openness between the partners. That is, to speak concretely, the church can learn from the world as well as the world from the church. The church is not to broadcast from a soundproof room, but to listen as well as speak. The premise for the lay apostolate, and the only basis for a sound dialogue, is a mature doctrine of creation. This means, among other things, that the Christian uses in the public forum a language appropriate to it: he does not, or should not, talk in the City as though he were speaking in the setting of the congregation (e.g., "we Christians," "this Christian nation," "all believing Americans," "all Christian citizens," "Christian America," etc.). In the secular setting he will speak a secular language.

Toward the end of the high Middle Ages, a man of insight wrote of the three great dialogues which impart wisdom: the dialogue with the Book of Life, Holy Scripture (the science of theology begins here); the dialogue with the Book of the World (the philosophy of the natural sciences begins here; as Francis Bacon put it at the beginning of modern science, nature must be "put to the question"); the dialogue with the past, which we call "History." The three dialogues are closely interrelated in the pursuit of wisdom. Two of them require special attention here.

In the dialogue with the Book of Life, Holy Scripture, we find repeated evidences that in Jewish and Christian belief the providence of God reaches out to all creation. Judaism is rarely sectarian. But speaking as a Christian may I point out that the first verses of the Gospel of John, in the Nativity story which parallels the more familiar passages in Luke (with the very human Jesus beginning as a babe lying in a manger), we find the One who was in the beginning with God portrayed as the Creator of all order. "All things were made by

Him; and without Him was not anything made that was made" (1:3). "He was in the world, and the world was made by Him" (1:10). The same message concerning the new Adam, the re-creator and restorer, appears in many places in the New Testament. In Ephesians we read how in the fullness of time he might "gather together in one all things in Christ" (1:10), and how the mystery of meaning "from the beginning of the world hath been hid in God, who created all things by Jesus Christ" (3:9). The most complete statement of all is found in a series of verses in the first chapter of Colossians, beginning a discussion of how all things were created by the One who is wisdom and truth, "in heaven, and that are in earth" (Col. 1:16). "And He is before all things, and by Him all things consist" (1:17).

Without plunging into the science of textual exegesis, may we agree on two major premises for those who take the New Testament seriously? First, the map on which action takes place is universal, indeed cosmological. Christianity is not a precious cult of pigmy truths known only to the illuminated, and applying only to a fragment of creation. Christianity claims the Saviour to be Creator as well, the law of love to be the law of life, the source of grace to be the source of all order and life. To claim that the redemptive process is limited to the Church is, from a Christian point of view, heretical. The Logos of God, the "hidden Christ," is working in secret ways to the redemption of the world. And there are many sons and daughters of the stranger, many who know not His name but bear the fruits of justice and righteousness, mercy and peace, who are being used of Him. This is assuredly the reason why Pope John addressed his great encyclical, *Pacem in Terris* (April 10, 1963), to "all men of good will."

The key question seems to me to be, however, how history

is viewed. It is quite foolish to think that one may approach history without presuppositions and come to "objective" conclusions which derive inexorably from the "facts." *Voraussetzungslose Geschichtswissenschaft* was impossible in Mommsen's own time, and it was never intended in the founding of the historical method by von Ranke. Ranke's basic concern —*wie es eigentlich gewesen sei*—was intended to give foundation to the dialogue with the past, not to stifle moral responsibility! The ocean of facts is infinite, and with the study of history, as in every other science, to get useful answers it is necessary to ask the right questions. What is the work of the Church across the generations? We are entitled neither to doctor the records nor to put our hands in our pockets and look on at life. The purpose of the Church, and the only occasion for its existence, is to be God's tool to the salvation of the world. To that end, the Church may be required, like her Lord, to die. To persist in preserving churchly life at the expense of the world; to insist that "secular" agencies and institutions must be drawn and drained "for the good of the Church"—these are the rationale of faithlessness and unbelief; this is the language of Christian imperialism rather than discipleship. Christian self-restraint directs us along another path entirely.

SECULARIZATION— THE CHURCH'S CONTRIBUTION

Across the centuries, a major work of the Church has been to aid the process of secularization. The Church, cultivating the mobility and discipline of a community of faithful people, has moved through the natural jungle, clearing and establishing areas of human dignity and liberty and order and turning them over to a world made aware. There was a time in Western Europe when only the Christians were concerned to rescue unwanted infants, exposed at night or sold into slavery by their parents. The Church founded rescue orders, established orphanages and homes. Today, in every civilized society this concern has been "secularized"; i.e., it has become a property or quality of the laws. In Hong Kong, where several dozen babies are exposed every night, church rescue missions still perform a necessary work. But should we regret that among more socially advanced societies social welfare work has become "secular"? One might think so considering the reluctance with which the churches give up their imbalanced financial commitments to orphanages, hospitals, and homes!

What of "secular" government? There was a time when all governments in Christendom enforced theological orthodoxy and liturgical conformity. Then there came a day when men began to perceive that—as William Penn put it—only that service is pleasing to God which is voluntary and uncoerced. In the fullness of time it was perceived that God was not honored by coercion and persecution. Reverence for the dignity of the human person required respect for conscience and for the internal integrity of dissenting religious communities as well as those teaching approved doctrine. A necessary complement to religious liberty and voluntaryism is "secular" government. The old governments of Christendom all claimed to be cathedrals; all asserted they served ultimate ends. Some still do, like the retrogressive and ideologically tainted governments of fascist or Communist countries. But in areas of liberty, government has been demythologized. "Secular" government, government of the kind that respects civic liberty—and religious liberty is different from toleration, which is merely prudential—knows its authority to be limited, knows itself to be a human invention for specific purposes, perceives its status to be—theologically speaking—"creaturely." Government that is modest and creaturely is a marvelous achievement in the history of human liberty.

Shall we seek to recede into the coercive past, with policies to implement some myth called "Christian America," some ideological slogan like, "America Back-to-God"; or shall we not, rather, rejoice in the blessings which are ours, as the sons and daughters of liberty, to be found in this time and place: America the World City, America the most magnificent area of ethnic and cultural and religious encounter and developing dialogue in the history of human kind?

Take higher education. In 1890 a high school education was a rare privilege and nine out of ten who enjoyed it graduated from private high schools. Then came the development of the public high school system. Is there anyone present who seriously regrets that we have entered an age when a high school education is enjoyed by the masses? Today we are well launched into a time of expanding higher education, when a college degree will soon be as common as a high school diploma was thirty years ago. The great load in this expansion of services has been carried by the state colleges and universities. Candor compels the admission that church and private colleges have not, so far, shown generosity of spirit toward this development. Where the private colleges did not for years actively oppose progress, as in Massachusetts, Connecticut and New York, they were at least guilty of neglect of good stewardship of their vocation. Harvard and Yale for decades fought every measure for expanding low-cost higher education in the legislatures of those states, and the colleges of upstate New York—engaged in educating an elite

—simply ignored the larger responsibility. Then, in the last few years, the pressure of parents and would-be students and the needs of the society grew so great that it could no longer be withstood. The State University of New York, with its 58 units—some of them anticipating 80,000 to 100,000 students per unit by 1980—and tremendous programs of expanded facilities and instructors, has in six short years become the largest university system in the world. Can any person of conscience, any person with a religious calling to stewardship over our youth resources, seriously desire a retrogression to the old situation?

Not at all! There was once a time when only a Christian church—in this case the Bohemian Brethren—advocated universal education of the youth. Then, in civilized countries, the principle was secularized. There was once a time when the modern institute of higher education—the first being the University of Paris, granted papal charters in 1219 and 1226 —emerged from the monastery and cathedral schools. There was once a time when, in the Protestant world, the founding of a college or university was part of every serious Reformer's program. The first Protestant university, Marburg, was chartered by Philip the Magnanimous of Hesse to implement the Reformation program announced in the Bad Homburg synod of 1526. In the fullness of time, however, the clearings carved out in the jungle by the Church have become secularized: What once only Christians and Jews saw to be a social need has now been accepted by the society at large. The record in America is the same: in the westward movement of the nineteenth century, the churches established academies and colleges almost as soon as government was there to grant articles of incorporation. And then, in the second half of the century, following on the high commitment fixed by the Morrill Land

Act (1862), the great secular college and university system began to gain strength.

Shall those of us who have made the religious commitment mourn that we are no longer solely in control, that higher education is now a mass undertaking rather than a privilege of the elite? Shall we resent and resist the very work which the "hidden Christ," the Logos of God, has been doing in history? Are we so blinded by heretical view of the created order that we can take pleasure only when good works are done by those plainly authorized to perform them? What a denial of love and liberty if we of the churches, our eyes securely fastened not on the Lord who gave men dignity but on the first mortgages we once held in the civilizing process, turn our backs on the mighty secular institutions which serve the society and—yes, let it be affirmed boldly—the Lord of History! The most grievous spiritual treason of which any person can be guilty is first to regret and then to deny the time and the place of his calling unto life.

The secular university, like secular government and secular social welfare in the secular city, is one of God's finest gifts to the liberty and dignity of the human person.

To illustrate the point, let us pursue the example of higher education further. If the secular university is a welcome development, what then (if any) is the role of the Christian college? If it no longer controls higher education, and the wrong-headed hope of impeding the development of secular education is doomed to defeat, why should the Christian college struggle to survive at all?

To ask this question is to look ahead rather than back, and since Christians are incurably future-oriented, let us risk prediction.

1. In the future, with the expansion of powerful and complex and essentially anonymous political and economic decision-making, the two-track system in higher education will be as vital to liberty as competition between the public and the private sectors in business, or checks and balances in government.

2. In the future, as the persons of technical proficiency our civilization requires are trained less in crash programs and pressure-cooker schemes, the contribution of the other pole of enlightenment—the pursuit of wisdom—will be more generally recognized. An educational system that stresses wisdom alone, without *Techne,* will end up a social fossil; an educational system that stresses technical proficiency alone and ignores wisdom (*Logos*), will turn out the most horrible figure of the modern age: the technically competent barbarian. The Amish case in Iowa illustrates the point. The Amish are much, much better and safer as neighbors than the men of the *Kripo* or the *Gestapo*—and safer than the scientists who serve the tyrants so uncritically! The Amish are, in fact, a good deal wiser about life's real meaning than are the technical experts in the Departments of Public Instruction of Iowa and Kansas, who seem so determined to persecute them. But the choice between education for life (archaic) and training in technical proficiency (barbarian) should not have to be made. Most of us believe that learning should encompass both wisdom and technics, and that the best way to keep both foci to the front and center is to keep an open and vigorous dialogue between the persons representing different educational histories and value systems. We may well covet for the dialogue between private colleges and state institutions the same open-faced, cordial, and creative

dialogue now enjoyed in our land between Catholics and Protestants, Christians and Jews. Often, however, the secularist ideologue has the most closed mind of all.

3. In the future, we shall see greatly increased cooperation between the state university systems and the private colleges. In many places, "cluster" colleges will develop, to make available to masses of students the richness of traditions and heritages which our varied backgrounds provide. Time was when the pious could fund colleges and seminaries out on the land, to protect their youth from pagan learning in the universities and temptation in the cities.[3] Today, with rapid transportation and instant communication, the ghettos and desert islands are caught up in the World City. The laws of gravity are bringing us together. For example, the 1963 White House Conference on the Role of Women heard a report that by 1971 at least half of a college education will be available by National Education Television. Not only the intellectual life of the young wife and mother locked to her residence will change; the whole geography of higher education is shifting, and the years immediately ahead will see major clusters of interinstitutional cooperation, including the building of complexes and faculties truly representative of the pluralism of the World City which America has become.

Other illustrations might be elaborated, but this should suffice. The "secular city," to which Harvey Cox called attention,[4] is—rightly conceived—a blessing and not a curse. The Christian ziggurats are being torn down. Sacral societies and monoliths, both old and new, are coming to be recognized for what they are: enemies of both high religion and the liberty and integrity of the created order.

There was once a time when persons of differing beliefs faced each other with the drawn knife. The day of toleration arrived, a kind of "cease fire" without appreciation of depth issues. There was once a time when established churches, controlling governments and universities and all major social institutions, limited full franchise to those who conformed. Then the day of liberty arrived, when men and women learned to separate the religious from the political covenant. In that day both the churches and the secular order were set free from coercion and manipulation. We are now moving beyond toleration and liberty to the dialogue which shall shape our future.

The system of liberty and self-government is far more sensitive than authoritarian systems. The absolute monarch or dictator has little need of the good will of his subjects, and no use for their initiative. But where there are *citizens,* they will honor those in authority and the liberties and dignities and reputations of those with whom they share a common destiny.

There may be those whose minds are tormented by ideology, who would gladly retrogress to the sacral government of Christendom or the fascist and Communist totalitarianism. Those who love liberty will look ahead and pray for secular government precisely *because* it is limited and creaturely. There may be those to whom Christianity is an ideology, who can conceive of education being useful only when it functions as a high-level school of confirmation or catechetical training. (Some dogmatic secularists, having failed to note that a truly secular university is precisely the place of liberty where genuine alternatives can meet in dialogue, think this way of the university.) But the essential business of the campus—as the trustees of St. John's in Manhattan and Drew at Madison have apparently forgotten—is a full, free, and informed dialogue in every department of science, from astronomy through history and theology to zoology. Let the dialogue flourish, and let the timorous and the ideologically closed minds flee, for in the Republic of Learning the Spirit who grants liberty and dignity shall prevail.

For the secular order to progress requires a rich doctrine and practice of stewardship—the discipline of life, talents, time, and effort in a vocational way. Precisely because we are passing out of a monolithic Christendom into a frank acceptance of pluralism—at least as a *Zwischenstadion*—it is imperative that each of the vocational communities develop a strong standard of self-discipline and service. The doctor is intended of God to be a steward of the public health—and not a member of a gang of bandits marked and marred by avarice. The teacher is intended of God to be a steward of the transmission of culture and learning—and not a tool of school politicians and so-called "human engineers." The policeman is intended of God to be a steward of the public order and trust—and not a brutalizer of the public. Not without cause are the fascist and Communist systems called "police states." According to the Bible, the place where those who are given authority over violence and use it not to protect the helpless but to torment them is called "Hell."

Where a profession or lay vocation is lacking in a structure and atmosphere of self-discipline, it will—being without the controls of earlier hierarchical societies—very speedily decline to the ethos of the jungle. A system of representative government is a higher form of political life than a despotism, to be sure; but an absolute monarchy is far better than popular sovereignty where the citizens have forgotten that the other side of the coin of liberty is self-discipline and self-restraint.

For the secular order to progress requires Christian self-restraint. How often the pulpits in the suburbs proclaim the monstrous notion that the trouble with the city is that sufficient "spiritual" influence is lacking in the Council! Then, once every generation (perhaps) a reform campaign is put forward to get selected candidates on the City Council. Such an effort may have merit, but only if the reform slate is chosen among all who have caught a vision of the City Just and Beautiful. If the reform slate is chosen on the basis of some idea of "Christian America," or worse yet in the mood to reconstruct some mythological past, the direction is wrong and the impact is wrong. What our liberty as a people requires is Christian self-restraint—an abandonment of Christian imperialism. The *polis,* the *Obrigkeit* (at various levels), the *universitas,* the layman's *vocatio* (*Beruf*) are to be respected in their integrity and deferred to in their dignity and liberty.

What I am saying, essentially, is this: we must span the bow more tensely, to build up a true Church for a real world. The old culture-religion was neither "religious" enough to be faithful, nor "secular" enough to be worthy of respect. It was a mishmash corruptive of both. The effort in some areas to preserve "Christendom" and in others to establish some new sacral (ideological) society is wrong-headed and reactionary. Specifically, the Marxist state (like the Nazi or fascist) is not "progressive": it is hopelessly retrogressive. We need, within the Church, a renewal of commitment, a surge of devotion to the life of the community of faithful people. We need, in the civil society, a resolute abandonment of all Christian colonialism and imperialism—coupled with a determination to work loyally with all men of good will in whom the love of justice and peace and mercy and righteousness has been awakened.

In the day of lay response, persons of religious commitment will be known, not for their anxiety toward creation, not for their fear of the created order, but for their generosity of heart and readiness of service.

▶7
THE RECOVERY OF CHRISTIAN INTEGRITY

AMID the pleasures and comforts of culture-religion, with the statistical successes attendant upon mass evangelism and social acceptance, the larger American churches have given less and less attention to membership standards. Yet the future of religion in America does not lie with a harmonism of prevailing creeds or opinions, any more than it lies with the sullen repetition of old words that no longer communicate. It lies with the recovery and the renewal and the transmutation of Christian discipline. Judaism might continue as a kind of social fossil, although the openness of our society has put the question of voluntary discipline to rabbis and elders in a way never felt before. The Jews, under religious liberty, can no longer rely upon the meanness of the "Christian world" to force identity upon them. Catholicism might continue and even grow in the traditional way, its message and style carried by "the religious," although it would be hard to turn the clock back in American Catholicism. But Protestantism cannot survive without a large measure of lay participation and conscious, disciplined action by the membership as a whole. This means that for Protestantism—today, by and large, so fully blended with prevailing cultural norms—the issue for the future lies between renewal and extinction.

In the modern world, "discipline" is a minus word and "freedom" is a plus word. Like many false polarizations, this scale of values, and the views of politics and church life based upon it, merely confuses the issue. The live alternative to despotism or totalitarianism is not anarchy: it is self-government. The jungle is never a true alternative to order. The self-discipline of free citizens is the only viable alternative to the voiceless and often reluctant obedience of subjects. Similarly, within the area of religious concern and practice the alternative to an authoritarian system is not individualism. It is an open covenant voluntarily arrived at. The priesthood of all believers does not mean, "every man his own priest": it means that within the covenant of faithful people, in the church's ministry to which each Christian is called in the ordination of his baptism, we have accepted "unlimited liability" one for the other. This is precisely what it means to be free in Christ: that I am not free to do as I please, but am called to be a servant of the servants of God.

Since men cannot live without order, and will turn to a tyrant rather than long endure chaos and the law of the jungle, the alternative to establishment—i.e., a church controlled by government or by culture—is the voluntary covenant. The individual who proclaims and practices anarchy is not a friend of liberty at all: he is a subverter and destroyer. The person who resists the yoke of Christ and church discipline is not an enemy of authoritarianism: rather, he is undermining the only viable alternative to it.

I am convinced that the noticeable wastage of some of our better college and seminary students from the revival churches to the Anglican and Lutheran communions is not primarily aesthetic at all, but due to the fact that these bodies have at least a church order and a sacramental life. Our fathers went out from them because the earlier established churches lacked the vigorous discipline of a covenantal community; now some of our children return because church discipline has fallen into disuse in our midst, and two years of catechetical instruction or six months of confirmation training are far better than nothing at all.

How far have we fallen, then, from the practices of the years when our fathers' restitution of the New Testament church included the distinction between catechumen and full member. In my own denomination, until the 1908 General Conference, *The Discipline* provided for a period of probation. A candidate was trained weekly for at least six months of preparatory membership before he could even be recommended for admission to full status. Today he can join with little or no preparation, and his name cannot be stricken from the rolls for years, regardless of how faithless he may prove to be! [1]

Responsible leaders in other denominations raise the same issue. Professor Findley Edge of Southern Baptist Theological Seminary urges in his lively book *A Quest for Vitality in Religion* that "some kind of waiting period" be introduced between the moment of decision on a person's part and his full admission.[2] In the age of the church struggle, church membership is too serious a matter to be dealt with frivolously. Nothing is more urgently needed today than the recovery of strong procedures for training God's people to the basic terms of reference in their ministry.

ARE STRUCTURES NECESSARY?

What is the relationship of internal church order to one's commitment to religious liberty? Is religious liberty necessarily in conflict with Christian discipline? For spiritualizers, the problem is simple: an individualistic attitude to the civil covenant is matched by unwillingness to yield to any yoke of obedience within the community of faith. Caspar Schwenckfeld insisted over four hundred years ago, writing from this point of view, that it is just as wrong to have spiritual coercion of the individual conscience in the church as it is to have princes and town councils controlling matters religious. The Ban is just as bad as burning: both involve coercion where freedom should rule. Within the last few years Duncan Howlett, American Unitarian, has argued that a true respect for religious liberty can be held only by individuals who reject both outward and inward coercion of belief.[3] From such a point of view, church discipline would be neither necessary nor desirable. A "free church" would thus be a religious association which is free of external controls or pressures and is only loosely held together within. The individual is thus "free" from both political coercion and ecclesiastical discipline.

A like question, often encountered, is whether an authoritarian ecclesiastical structure can function as a "free church." Does a communion with an internal order based on absolute monarchy, or perhaps a "collegiality" of episcopal *imperia*, of necessity jeopardize the religious liberty of all? The fathers of the Free Churches certainly believed so, and they condemned a prideful and power-conscious hierarchy as vigorously as they denounced persecuting governments. They were using in both cases the test of the early church, and neither powerful hierarchs nor worldly princes controlled Christian decisions then.

But certainly there is a theological issue here, too, as well as a question of historical interpretation. The Protestant attitude to ecclesiastical institutions (among other human associations) has ever kept before our eyes the warning that unless we are faithful in our structures as well as individually the Kingdom may be taken from us and given to a people bringing forth fruits meet for repentance. We are warned that He is able of the very stones to raise up children of Abraham (Matt. 22:43; Luke 3:8). It may well be that power can become so institutionalized in the church, as well as in society at large, and individuals become so situated as to seek defensively its unquestioned maintenance, that the institution's own claims become a major denial of the grace of Christian liberty.

The practical effect of an authoritarian church structure may be to train ordinary men and women to docility and submission rather than to the commitment and initiative we look for in an enlivened laity. In the civic sense, however, a "free church" can have papal, episcopal, presbyterial, collegiate, synodical, or congregational polity. The person who is free to leave without political or legal penalty is also at liberty to choose the terms of his religious obedience. And it is within the context of "obedience" that the liberty of a Christian man must finally be defined, whatever the methods by which standards are attained to.

Here we come to the flaw in the reasoning of the spiritual-izers. For to be "free" in Christ is not to be without responsibility to the Law and to the brethren: on the contrary, it is to accept within the church's ministry an unlimited liability for one's cobelievers. The temporal end of our liberty is the covenant, not anarchy. And the true alternative to coercion is not anarchy, but order which is "talked up" and freely maintained by free men. That is, the voluntary covenant is the alternative to tyranny—not the jungle.

Thus the Christian men of liberty, in their principle of church government, have found a way between the two most common errors of the contemporary church—both of them well known in the early period as well: Monophysitism and Docetism. The extreme Catholic doctrine of the mystical body of Christ, in which the church is interpreted as an extension of the second person of the Trinity, represents the one error.[4] Practically, it is impossible to criticize an institution thus directly identified with divine perfection—and doubtless this has been the occasion of the concept's usefulness to the more authoritarian prelates. It tends to silence criticism. Equally dangerous is the second error: abuse of the familiar distinction between "visible" and "invisible" church. For the Great Reformers, this scholastic and nonbiblical distinction was necessary because of the way in which the Protestant state churches were very early fragmented. This was the one device by which, in the midst of the extremes of particularity and captivity, the concept of a Church Universal— though hidden—could be maintained. But the end result has been a docetic church view, in which the connection between the "heavenly" church and the "worldly" church has been almost totally lost.

The church seems to proclaim that in the Universal Church

there is brotherhood, but in the earthly community there is social and racial segregation. The church proclaims that there is a Christian style of life, but in the concrete situation the Christians act just like the other Gentiles. This is a type of the heresy of Docetism, and it should not be seen among churches alive in their liberty. For classical Christianity knows no convenient escape mechanism such as the distinction between the "visible" and the "invisible" church: it knows only the disciplines of discipleship and the structures of service. The key word is "witness." It is witness—the affirmative dimension of religious liberty—which gives integrity and meaning to the Christian movement. Ultimately, the church is freed for the sake of service not for apostasy.

Toleration can be defined exclusively in a negative way as "freedom *from*," and here the confusion arises. The persistent tendency of the individual to think of discipline in relationship to himself and his own restrictions, rather than in relation to Christ and what service we owe Him, is the reason why many still confuse toleration with religious liberty. Nevertheless, the two are not the same. Undoubtedly, with the long tradition of toleration in England, the average person there is convinced that he enjoys religious freedom. If he is Baptist or Congregationalist or Wesleyan, for example, his actual experience will be little different from that enjoyed by cobelievers in the United States. In fact, however, the structure of church life in England is quite different from what we know here. In spite of the freedom of dissent guaranteed at law since the 1689 Act of Toleration, he lives in a society whose religious atmosphere is largely fixed by an established church. The Church of England is privileged by acts of Parliament, especially the Act of Uniformity of 1662, and the rest are accordingly disinherited. The rejection by

Parliament of the revised Prayer Book in 1927 and 1928 demonstrated that the spiritual life of the Church of England is not controlled by its communicants. The procedure followed in the appointment of bishops accentuates the dependent relationship, as does the fact that approximately one-fourth of the "livings" of Anglican clergy are still directly subject to patronage by the lords of manor.

If the individual is thinking only of his own freedom, he will scarcely notice a difference between England and America. But if he has in mind the larger dimensions of religious liberty, those matters without which liberty would never have been attained and without which it will not long continue, he will perceive immediately that the Church of England has neither covenant nor discipline and that England has toleration and not liberty.

The case is much the same with the churches in West Germany. The growth of an attitude of toleration and good will in former Protestant establishments can be traced in the shift of the German Lutheran churches from state church to territorial church to *Volkskirche*. Yet, for all of the humane advance evident in the dismantling of earlier patterns of behavior, the price of privilege is still being paid. The men of the movements of renewal, such as the *Kirchentag* and the Evangelical Academies, are much concerned for the recovery of apostolic church life through lay initiative, missions as a responsibility of the whole church, *Kirchenzucht* (church discipline), *Kerngemeinde* (the gathered minority of the faithful), etc. The establishments themselves, as can readily be discerned in their system of theological education, still pay the price of a mixed commitment. Their pastors are trained in state institutions, at tax expense, and in the last generations they have made two fatal, and symbolic, blunders. First, dedicated to pure science, they lost the confidence of the devout in the churches; the *Kirchliche Hochschulen* were founded in protest. Second, following World War II, dedicated to rigidly professional concerns, they abandoned the problems of the whole people; the Evangelical Academies, with their own research centers and staffs in theology, were founded separate from them to fill the vacuum. In both cases, the continuation of old traditions ensured that new life and renewal had to develop separate from the official centers of institutional leadership. But in America voluntaryism affords a wide area for experimentation and exploration with new structures of witness in the church itself. Structures are indeed necessary, but set in the context of Christian faithfulness and not imposed from without.

The tradition of two vital but separate covenants requires vigorous self-discipline by the church; it also requires a conscious self-restraint on the part of government. Even the courts have from time to time reverted to the old practice of meddling in the internal affairs of churches. This was of course standard procedure in earlier centuries, when religious and civic rights were hopelessly confused, but with the rise of religious liberty and Free Churches the judiciary has been learning to respect the *potestas ecclesiae*. A central premise of religious liberty is, after all, that church discipline is attained and maintained within the church—without deference to or interference from the political authorities. But there are throwbacks from time to time, and one occurred recently in connection with a disciplinary case of the Mar Vista Baptist Church in Los Angeles.

In this incident, it is reported that after a quarrel with other women of the congregation in connection with a wedding reception, Mrs. John A. Chapman proceeded to attempt to break up the Sunday morning worship. She sang deliberately off key, talked loudly during services, and insisted on taking communion while under suspension (classically, "the lesser Ban"). Her husband and daughter became involved, and finally the congregation had to rebuke and dismiss all three from the covenant (classically, "the greater Ban"). At this point they went to court, and Superior Court Judge Mc-Intyre Faries reversed the congregation's action. Pastor Wayne P. Eurich and the congregation of Mar Vista Baptist Church are thus under constraint not to function as a Free Church, their obedience to Matthew 18:15–19 reversed by a court which has no business in the affair one way or another.[5] The particulars of the case cannot be established at this distance, nor are they relevant.

There is no natural or civic right to belong to a congregation's covenant, and the only proper action for a court in such a case is to declare itself without jurisdiction. The common understanding of religious liberty is so vague, however, that the judge evidently lacked the most elemental understanding of the nature of the Free Church. Even among the baptized there are many who confuse state policy with church policy, toleration with liberty, individualism with the priesthood shared by all believers.

WHAT DISCIPLINE?

The previous incident was chosen to illustrate the critical nature of the problem of discipline, and the need to resolve specific issues at the level of congregational policy rather than at the level of statist ideology. For religious liberty to flourish requires both Christian self-restraint and self-restraint by government.

We cannot implement religious liberty by holding to the rule of hostility to the church: anticlericalism has in the modern period simply cleared the way for more violent and intolerant ideologies than even coercive state churches. We cannot find our way by hostility to the state: this stance has at least more Christian history behind it than the other, but it is ill-fitted to the American scene where every free citizen shares with his fellows in the political sovereignty. No, in the purely descriptive sense our system of religious liberty can be called one of friendly separation between the political covenant and the religious covenants. The rule of thumb for specific decisions in the field is this: does the action enhance the freedom of the church to be the True Church, or does it pull downward toward the old and familiar uses and misuses of religion for low-level purposes? Does the action honor the integrity of secular, limited government, or does it slide toward coercion of conscience?

It takes more than accurate description to maintain religious liberty. It requires more than careful definition. Even the courts cannot permanently maintain our liberties if the will to voluntaryism and responsible self-discipline has wasted away beyond recovery. And when the liberty at stake is religious liberty, then it must be stated quite bluntly that the positive foundation of our liberty rests upon the covenant and upon church discipline.

The goal for the church is the clear calling to that level of religion which brings forth the willing devotion of time and money and life itself. The purpose of religious liberty and separation is to make that quality of religion possible. Such religion as this, neither persecuted nor patronized by government, neither manipulating government nor neglecting the responsible service of loyal citizens, emerged historically in

America: it is America's greatest contribution to date to human liberty. Religious liberty will not long survive a decline and fall of vigorous, voluntary church covenants. The guarantee of our liberty is the disciplined life of a faithful and willing people. The most urgent need is that we carry forward with faith and vigor the prayer cells, lay academies, new style of mass dialogue, and other movements of lay renewal which will give a new meaning and content to that discipline. In the long haul, it is the positive phase of religious liberty that is most important, the determination of the religious communities to use their freedom to a constructive end. "Cooperative separatism" will only function where both communities, the baptized and the secular, are aware of their limitations and their true functions.

THE CHURCH FOR THE NEW AGE

When we speak of the mission of the Church in the world, and the life of a covenant people fulfilling God's plan for them in the world, we immediately perceive a tension between "the Church" and "the world." What the Christians hold dear is not always what the world treasures. What the Christians look forward to is not what the world longs for. We are apt to misunderstand this tension between the Church and the world, to conceive of it as a fixed hostility. Then we find it hard to understand how "God so loved the world" when we Christians are supposed to shun "the world, the flesh, and the devil."

The solution to the puzzle lies in closer study of what the Bible means when it speaks of "Church" and "world." The Greek word which was translated "world" is even more appropriately translated "the spirit of the times" or simply "aeon" or "age." This "world" is not a fixed entity, in which Christians live a kind of fortress existence amidst hostile territory. Neither is the work of evangelism to conduct sorties from time to time into the enemy camps, bringing back occasional scalps (called "conversions"). The "world" which we are to shun is the dying age upon which the judgment of God has already been passed. The "Church" is that people which has been called out to train for life in the New Age, the age which is coming into being. The Christians are, as it were, citizens of the Kingdom who now have their first papers. Now they are in the encampment from time to time to train to be better equipped soldiers of Christ (*milites Christi*), to be stronger athletes of the Spirit, to be fit citizens for the coming City of God.

The world is seen in two different ways, and here is the confusion. There is the "world" which is the age that is passing away, and there is the "world" which is the created order that even now God is redeeming. When the "new breed" of theologians speak enthusiastically of "a world come of age" they mean the created order which is being reclaimed and restored. (Their occasional use of "ecstatic utterance" should not confuse us: Christians have often spoken with tongues in times of renewal.) To embrace the style and life of the age which is passing away, however, the world which is dying, is to "choose death."

A major source of our problem is that we have not perceived as clearly as our fathers the necessary tension between the "Church" which is the people of the New Age and the "world" which is the age that is dying. The world that is passing away is the world of warring, lust, the dehumanization of persons, the exploitation of the helpless, the murder of the defenseless, the wicked rule of anarchy and the jungle. The world which is being called into being is the Kingdom of God, of which we have a foretaste in the Church. When organized religion accepts the norms of the dying age, that is, when it is no longer truly the Church of Jesus Christ, there is of course no taste at all. The "saltiness" is lost. The Church has then blended into a flat, tasteless culture-religion. But when the Church is truly a faithful people, when this people is true to its calling, its fellowship in mission and ministry is glorious. This faithful community may be scorned or persecuted by the dying age, but its joy in the God who keeps His promises is secure.

The Church consists, then, of those persons who are citizens-in-training. They see themselves as a people subject to the Lord "to whom all power has been given in heaven and on earth." He is the Lord of love, brotherhood, mercy, sympathy, pure human relations. He is the Lord of the Kingdom described in Isaiah and in Revelation, the Kingdom which is simply the return of the created order to that perfection for which God purposed it. They do grievous wrong, and deny the truth of the Bible, who seek to limit His Lordship to purely individual or family religion. The God of the Bible is no Confucianist household god, to be pulled out of the corner for private occasions: He is the Lord of the world (the created order) which sometimes resists His will so resolutely, just as He is the Head of the Church (the people of the New Age) where His coming victory is already being celebrated.

TWO KINDS OF LAY TRAINING

To live in tension, in spiritual warfare, with the dying age requires training. We learn to "think with the mind of Christ." We learn to cultivate and proclaim a style of life which the "world" (the dying age) of warring, racism, dehumanization, and exploitation hates and seeks to destroy. The agents of rebellion, "the princes and powers of this world's darkness," usually practice anonymity and facelessness, but they can be identified. More serious, however, is the penetration of the Church by the mind-set and style of "this world." To guard against this, and to turn the faithful community outward to service, the renewal movements of our time all stress the recovery of Christian discipline. Theology, liturgy, ethics, morals, a sound church order—all are involved in any genuine program of renewal.

We can neither settle for the isolation of the fortress, and let the created order go to the devil (as though *he* were the lord of the world), nor can we embrace without question the spirit and style of the age which is dying. We are called to be a *true* Church for a *real* world (created order), and to take both of these dimensions of God's work seriously.

There are two kinds of lay training being developed across the Christian world today, from Mindolo in the Copper Belt to Bad Boll in Germany to Iona in Scotland to Kirkridge in the Delaware Water Gap to Northern Hokkaido Christian Academy. Both are essential to the renewal of the Church and the reclaiming of the world (created order) for which Christ died. Neither—and this is the important point—is adequate without the other. First, there is lay training *in the church*. We desperately need laymen who know their Bible, church history, theology, who understand where the frontlines are found in Christian ethics and Christian mission. We need lay preachers, lay leaders—the second level of leadership in the church which keeps the wheels turning, which enlarges the preacher's limited reach. We need volunteers, and one of the most healthy aspects of American Christianity—in contrast to that produced in most of Europe—is the readiness of lay people to volunteer and get things done. Over a century and a half—in the YMCA, the Sunday school movement, and a dozen like initiatives—one of the most blessed things about American church life has been the willingness of the non-clergy to share in the church's ministry. But this is not enough, alone.

The second kind of lay training, the kind which has been developed so remarkably in the *Vormingscentren* of the Netherlands and the *Evangelische Akademien* of Germany, is lay training *in the world*. A wonderful part of lay renewal in postwar Europe has been the reclaiming of whole professional and vocational groups. These groups, the basic communities in industrial civilization, had been corrupted and demoralized during the Third Reich. When the war was over, men like Reinold von Thadden-Trieglaff, Hans Hermann Walz, Eberhard Mueller, Hans-Jakob Rinderknecht, Hans-Ruedi Weber, Hans-Rudolf Mueller-Schwefe, Hans Kallenbach, Erich Mueller-Gangloff, Horst Symanowski, Gerhard Heilfurth, and Willem Kist—encouraged and aided by theologians and churchmen like Emil Brunner, Ferdinand Sigg, Hendrik Kraemer, and Hanns Lilje—set out to redeem the times. They founded their work on one of the basic Reformation teachings: that a teacher or farmer or soldier or craftsman who does his daily work in the fear of God and love of his fellows is as truly one of "the religious" as any of the ordained. They took whole sections of the broken and demoralized society and reclaimed them, playing a basic role in the remarkable recovery which is so often, and falsely, discussed in purely economic terms. They did it by concentrating on the mission and witness of laymen in the world.

Example: The Vocation of Policemen. In Tutzing, the Evangelical Academy of the church in Bavaria, well over fifty

institutes have been held since 1947 for policemen. Twenty
years ago the German police were among the most depraved
thugs in the world. Today, they comprise one of the best
police forces to be found anywhere—polite toward civilians,
loyal to their government, obedient to the constitution and
bill of rights of the German republic. Nothing has contributed more to their redemption as a vocation than the
work of the lay institutes. State ministers of justice, ministers
of the interior, and often the longtime cabinet minister and
head of police Dr. Gerhard Schroeder, have participated in
these institutes for policemen.

Think of the vocational questions: What is law? What is
the cornerstone of justice? What do the churches owe policemen who are faithful to their calling? The early Christians,
subjects of a government far inferior to ours, said that if
policemen fulfilled their office-duty in the fear of God and
love of their fellows they were entitled not only to respect
but to the prayers of the churches. The Christians prayed
that they might do their duty and keep their hands from in-
nocent blood. That is still a good prayer for police forces.

What have we done recently in the American churches for
policemen? They fill an extremely important role in any society. They have the stewardship of law and order and keep
us from retrogressing to the jungle. Yet we have let them go,
without the churches' prayers, without Christian instruction,
kicked around by the politicians, underpaid, offered bribes
by unscrupulous businessmen—and then we are surprised
when some of them join the beasts of prey!

Example: The Vocation of Doctors. Consider the doctors,
so demoralized by the Hitler period. Even if they had not
participated personally in the terrible experiments on human
beings conducted in the Nazi murder camps, they were

informed: the results were published from time to time in the medical journals. After the war they could not sit down in a group and look each other in the eye. Then, under the leadership of the lay institutes, doctors and surgeons and hospital administrators and specialists were brought together to discuss their duty as persons of education and privilege in rebuilding society. Slowly and painfully the sense of stewardship and integrity was regained.

The doctor is a steward of the public health, just as the policeman is a steward of the public order. We can argue about the technicalities, what belongs to the private sector and what to the public. But that is purely incidental to the main issue: whether the doctor sees himself as a steward, called to a vocation, or whether he sees himself as an entrepreneur leagued with other bandits to take advantage of his fellow citizens. What have the churches in America done to clarify that?

Example: The Vocation of Schoolteachers. Consider the burden carried by the elementary-school teachers in our society: to explain the madness of the adult world to little children in such a way that they will not repudiate their heritage utterly. In some cities in America the schoolteacher has the most difficult vocation of all. Most little children are just like thoroughbreds: without any verbalization at all they sense and absorb like a blotter the anxieties and confusions of the adult world. And the teacher has the stewardship of the transmission of culture from generation to generation, working under such hazards.

What are we doing to help schoolteachers to fulfill their vocation?

Example: The Military Chaplaincy. The one major type of clergy service (in addition to some few in institutional chaplaincies or in the campus ministry) which is actually geared to the job to be done is the military chaplaincy. They live the common life with those they serve. They know the problems. They know the temptations and the limitations, and also the daily opportunities for faithful stewardship.

What we very much need in the rest of the church is a network of specialized group ministries, of persons who know the languages and the daily-life situations of the specialized communities of modern civilization. We need clergy who can be chaplains to laymen in the world's work, and laymen who are trained to witness and mission in the world.

THE EVANGELIZATION OF SOCIAL STRUCTURES

What is required is to break out of the ghetto of purely private piety, to take social structures seriously. It is amazing how capable and hard-headed men, men able to handle the food services and transportation and construction engineering of the Great City, will—when they enter the men's class on Sunday morning—so often forget everything they know. Well trained in their various specialized vocations, able to keep a highly complex network of services going, when they begin talking "the church language" they often revert to totally irrelevant individualistic and subjective terms.

In modern society we are utterly dependent upon groups of discipline or indiscipline whose members we will never know, whose daily decisions affect our health and life itself. That such structures fulfill their intended purpose is far more important, in most cases, than incidents of individual sin or virtue. Take this illustration of the point: Don Benedict, "Mr. Inner City" in America and founder or consultant to most of the important metropolitan works across the land, was walking down the street in East Harlem, New York City, one day. He saw a man struck by a car, lying in the gutter. The Good Samaritan would, of course, have tended him immediately, given him first aid, provided him with care for his wounds. But if you move an injured person on one of our city streets you go to jail. So he did what the law allowed: telephoned for an ambulance. Ambulance service being what it is, particularly to a poor section of town, the ambulance took an hour to get there and the man died on his way to the hospital. What is a Christian then to do? Suddenly it came to him: If you want to be a Good Samaritan in our kind of civilization you must work to improve the ambulance service! Most of the sins committed in our society are done by committee, and most of the good which is accomplished depends upon the faithfulness of vocational "peer groups." Until we have grasped that truth we have missed the point of who we are and where God has placed us in the world.

THE PASSING OF AGRARIAN CIVILIZATION

In an earlier period, Christian relationships were still defined largely in neighborly terms. The self-sufficient family farm was still important, and the old church language still communicated. Many readers will still remember grandfather's farm, where almost everything needed to live on was raised. He had lasts on which he did his own shoe repairing. He raised corn and ground it on a treadmill. He raised hens and put the eggs down in waterglass. The parsnips were put down in sunken barrels, the potatoes and onions into bins in the cellar. The only thing he had to buy was salt. Today that same farm—if not in the Soil Bank—is part of our agricultural industry, raising one crop. Across the whole country the base of agriculture has changed. We are not talking, therefore, in terms of a dichotomy between town and country. Dairy farmers, wheat farmers, corn growers, turkey raisers —all are just as much caught up in the complex relationships of the Great City as those of us who work on the assembly line or in the company offices downtown. We are all today dependent upon vocational "peer groups" within which ethical conduct and stewardship are cultivated or within which the law of the jungle flourishes, with never the light of the gospel penetrating the darkness.

Once the function of high religion was to give sacramental character to the natural community of family and covenant. Later it was to ennoble the neighborly relationships of agrarian civilization. Today it is to declare the meaning of the new relationships, primarily vocational, primarily defined by social role. In the society at large we need the "tents," the new types of parish, fitted to the needs and possibilities of the real world.

"BETWEEN THE TIMES"

Characteristic of our situation is the fact that we live "between the times." Most of the old ways of doing things are losing authority, and so far we have made only a beginning in developing the style of Christian witness appropriate to the New Age. With the end of Christendom, with the end of "parish" and "congregation" and even "seminary" as we have previously understood them, much is cast loose. With America's religious liberty and voluntaryism creating a relationship between free churches and a free society such as has never before existed anywhere, much of our doctrinal and institutional posture is simply outdated.

What is a "parish"? This medieval concept still makes it possible for Continental churches to define their basic unit geographically. The Luther Church in Frankfurt Main includes all the souls not Catholic between certain streets north and south and certain parallel streets running east and west. What does that mean in Chicago, where persons drive past half a dozen or more churches to find the one they want to affiliate with?

What is a "pilgrim congregation"? This Free Church concept has come to mean the right to make pilgrimage out of the central city into the suburbs, to let the inner city go to rot. Perhaps there has always been a "split-level fellowship" in the church, as Wesley Baker suggests.[6] But what we must have is a large number of experimental ministries, both ordained and unordained, until we have discovered some new and more viable ways of getting at the matter of the church's mission. This is what the new centers represent, from the Lay School of Theology at Anderson, South Carolina, through Kirkridge to Yokefellow and the Glide program on the West Coast. Neither should we forget the Chicago Ecumenical Institute and the Chicago City Missionary Society (now the Church Renewal Society), with their various ministries. We need to learn from each other. It is a good laboratory where one out of fifty experiments proves out. Rather than viewing these radical experiments with alarm, we should embrace them with our prayers and our dialogue and our support. Nothing that any of them can do will be as scandalous as to maintain business-as-usual in a world aflame.

FOUR LEVELS OF BREAKTHROUGH
IN LAY TRAINING

Across the Christian world there seem to be four significant breakthroughs in lay training.

First, there is a strong upsurge of emphasis on small-group work. They are variously called fellowship groups, prayer cells, "class meetings" (the original Wesleyan term), house churches, circles. This is the optimum unit for rapid learning and mobility of witness. The small, personal, primary group is where most real learning occurs. My colleague, Philip Anderson of Chicago Theological Seminary, has summarized the imperative of association in this way:

> We have been *formed* by the groups to which we belonged in the past; we can be *transformed* by the groups to which we belong in the future. One example of this transforming power of the small group is the change in an adolescent when he leaves the family group and joins his fellow teenagers. The history of the Church is filled with examples of the transforming power of small groups—Jesus and his disciples, Wesley and his meetings, the Pilgrims, and many of the small group beginnings of present-day denominations.
>
> If we could provide an equally significant belonging for our church members today, we could transform the Church.[7]

Second, there is the breakthrough involving vocational and peer groups. Here we find the best of the campus ministries. Here is the deep lode in which the evangelical academies and lay institutes are working. Steelworkers, lawyers, even preachers, find the context of their real life in these specialized communities in the complex modern society. This point has been elaborated at length already.

Third, there are the "evangelical communities," as Donald Bloesch calls them.[8] These are the new orders and group ministries: Taizé in France, Iona in Scotland, East Harlem Protestant Parish, the team of the Chicago Ecumenical Institute, Reba Place Fellowship, etc. This style of work is sometimes developed in the larger parish on the land. In the Great City, especially, the recovery of Christian discipline calls for communities of particular vocation.

The new orders that serve in the inner city have even taken to wearing simple dress again. There is rarely the chance to verbalize, to preach. What is involved is the witness of being present (*L'Apostolat de la Présence*). The men of East Harlem used sometimes to sit in meetings of social welfare and social service representations numbering fifty or sixty agencies in north Manhattan. They were the only ones who actually lived there. The other delegates were all commuting in from Long Island or Westchester County to do good for people. By their presence and by their rule of life such group ministries "say" something very important: community is possible. The one rule that every youngster learns in the jungle of the city streets, the one rule that every dopie and ex-con knows by heart, is this: "Don't trust anyone!" Don't trust the teacher. Don't trust the caseworker. Don't trust the cop. Don't trust the members of your own gang. Don't trust your parents. Finally, the broken man becomes an isolate, a fragmented person. And these are they to whom the Order, with its simple style of life and its discipline, declares reconciliation and acceptance. "You're wrong: in Christ, community is found."

Fourth, there is the new style of "saturation evangelism." In the *Kirchentag*, Kirk Week, the Faith-in-Life Dialogues at Fargo-Moorhead and Duluth-Superior and the Twin Cities a new kind of mass impact on metropolitan areas is being developed. Every possible medium is used, chiefly by lay volunteer groups, to reach everyone in a given area at least once in the week *on his own wavelength*. We have learned enough now in this country and abroad to see that this kind of a massing of effort is the new style of mass evangelism, just as the camp meeting was the style a century ago.

THE GOLDEN AGE OF THE FAITH

To talk of "the age of the laity" makes some of us clergy nervous. At Bad Boll, the great Lay Institute near Stuttgart, they found after seven years that unless they had institutes for clergy there was no point in training the laity at all. The last thing on earth the old-style clergy wanted was an aroused laity. They just clutter up the field and confuse the promotional program!

A seminary president, a man whom I have loved and admired for many years, said to me some months ago: "Frank, you young fellows make me nervous talking about an aroused laity. In my experience, when the laity gets aroused it's usually on the wrong side! I think it's better to let sleeping dogs lie." This still seems to me a singularly unbrotherly way of referring to the unordained.

The truth is that a new and renewed laity requires a new kind of clergy. You even have to have a new kind of seminary. The point is this: the present wave of renewal movements throughout the Christian world is putting the question to all of us—to the Church as well as to the world. That of the Church which clings to the dying age will be axed. That of the world which serves hatred and warring and racism and dehumanization will pass away. In Christ a New Age is introduced. A new people is being gathered. The created order is being restored. A new discipline of life and thought is emerging.

There are some who like to think of "the good old days." They long for the fourth century, that great age of creeds officially settled and enforced, when bishops beat each other over the heads with staves and theologians consigned each other to eternal damnation. Others long for the sixteenth century, that great age of the Formula of Concord and the Council of Trent and the Synod of Dort, when Protestant and Catholic Reformers condemned each other in batches and cooperated only in burning and hanging the Anabaptists. Others seem to long for the "good old days" of the Founding

Fathers of "Christian America," when Negroes knew their place, women could not vote, and ordinary folk called their betters "Mister."

In truth, we live in better times! In the fullness of time God has given us a people who are willing and eager to do volunteer work in the Church's ministry. If we who are called to lead do our job, this time of lay renewal will introduce one of the most glorious renaissances in the history of the faith. And the formlessness, the lack of style, which now dishonors the Name and confuses the observers will be replaced by new structures of Christian discipline.

▶8
A
TEACHING
CHURCH

PROTESTANTS have been accustomed since the Reformation to emphasize *preaching*. Since the success of home missions and the revival movements of the nineteenth century, the Church's work in *proclaiming* has been generally conceded. Strange as it seems to our Jewish neighbors, to whom the rabbi is above all "teacher," or to our Catholic neighbors, for whom the Church is above all *Magistra* in dealing with matters of faith and morals, Protestants have come slowly and reluctantly to the responsibility of *teaching*. The criticism is directed with less validity to Lutheranism, with its catechetical tradition, and to Anglicanism, with its training for Confirmation; but in radical Protestantism, at least, the teaching role of the Church has been neglected. The excuses have been many. If the individual has been truly converted he will find the necessary guidance in his conscience. Let the word be limited to the Simple Gospel, without complicated applications or involved relevances. Catholicism may stress community controls, but Protestantism owns the creed of individualism.

All of these rationalizations are nonbiblical, of course, since they deny the New Testament understanding of the Church as a community of faithful people. As the martyr Dietrich Bonhoeffer put it (and he too was faced by those who excused their apostasy by reference to individual autonomy): "I have no control over freedom as over a property. It is simply the event that happens to me through the other." [1] There is no freedom without *free for*. All personhood is realized through community. There is no relationship to Christ, the Head of the Church, except through the faithful community. There are those who proclaim a purely spiritual fellowship, apart from the ugly and earthy compromises of the real. They believe there is "a danger of confusing and mixing the two spheres, whereas there can be no such danger in a purely spiritual fellowship. This idea, however, is a great delusion. According to all experience the truth is just the opposite. . . . A purely spiritual relationship is not only dangerous but also an altogether abnormal thing." [2] True discipleship requires a corporate witness.

No corporate witness is possible without *formation* (to use the excellent word of the Catholic lay apostolate). "Teaching" has all too long meant a schooling of the merely intellectual, as though orthodoxy of belief could excuse a heresy of life. When we speak of a "teaching church," therefore, and when we accent the office of the minister as teacher, we are not referring to intellectual assent or rectitude alone. We mean the formation of men and women made new in Jesus Christ into the persons God intends them to be. The Christian community, when being renewed, is known as much by its style of life as by the soundness of its doctrine. As John Doberstein pointed out, Bonhoeffer's life of thought and action was "a turning away from the phraseological to the real." [3] We who have survived one stage of the Church struggle, and are called to spiritual warfare in another stage, can learn from him how life in Christ is "being a part of the one, holy, Catholic, Christian Church, where it shares actively and passively in the sufferings and struggles and promise of the whole Church." [4]

In his excellent address at the World Conference on Church and Society (Geneva, 1966), Professor Wendland of Münster spoke of the Church's proper role as a force in a revolutionary age: "The Church itself becomes the source of constant revolutionary changes in state and society. Rooted as it is in the eschatological-revolutionary power of the Christian message, the Church's attitude to the historical revolution is both positive and critical." [5] The Church must not only oppose all Utopian ideologies, but also provide models of effective action which are applicable to the life of the larger society. This has been the historic mission of the Church, redeeming the world, to clear areas in the jungle of human sin, within which models can be built and later "secularized" (i.e., applied to the life in the world). Bishop Otto Dibelius of Berlin brought out the Church's responsibility to provide models in his fine discussion of the Christian encounter with Nazism and Communism, *Grenzen des Staates*. It is not enough for the Church to preach truth: it must also demonstrate alternative forms of order.[6] Beyond this, the Church creates order where previously chaos had ruled.

BUILDING MODELS

We reject phraseology which is not backed by disciplined action. We reject "orthodoxy" of language which is not supported by orthodoxy of life. The New Testament itself is explicit enough. But apart from such reference, important to Christians, the social psychologists and sociologists of knowledge have made perfectly clear that what is really taught and learned, in the area of ultimate concerns if not in technics, is that which is modeled rather than that which is verbalized. The chief reason so many bright young people have no use for organized religion, although they are excited about theology as an intellectual discipline and about service in the inner city, is that they believe churchmen are hypocrites and church conferences and agencies hypocritical: churchmen talk a good game, but their actions (or lack of them) show what they really mean. The young people react against the discrepancy between façade and reality. Later they may accommodate and live the schizophrenic life of great masses of the baptized, splitting carefully the archaic church language and high principles of Sunday morning from the vernacular and "common sense" of daily living. In the meantime, however, they are revolted. The chance the churches have with young people and students, like their chance with lay people who take things seriously, depends upon our openness to experimentation, new forms of service, models of credible witness. The problem of the churches is the "credibility gap" which exists between a verbalization that lays all weight on selfless service and a policy that devotes most attention to statistical reports and building programs.

Since we live "between the times," with dialogue and experimentation the orders of the day, any models put forward must have a consciously tentative nature. They must conceive of themselves as contributions to the Christian movement rather than final answers. We do not need the erection of new Christian ziggurats to replace the old proud towers, but rather the faithful covenants of volunteers. The cutting edge of the Christian movement is pressed by "the Church in motion" (slogan of the 1949 *Kirchentag*), by the Church which sees itself again a "pilgrim people." [7] To live in tents calls for the greatest devotion and discipline, and it is difficult for those who have pledged their lives, fortunes, and sacred honor to a cause to avoid claiming more quality for their position than it in fact possesses. To be able to do this calls for the risk of faith. Nothing new is brought forth into the world unless it is loved more than it deserves to be loved. But a brotherly and charitable attitude on the part of the Christians can both encourage experimentation and help prevent pretentiousness among those spiritual outsiders who carry the battle and the heat of the day before the main enemy is engaged.

It is dangerous to write down and recommend models, for premature exposure can corrupt the experiment before the reports are in and sound conclusions can be drawn. There is a general feeling among the experts in new methods of lay training that a number of promising programs and projects in European and American churches since World War II have been ruined precisely by being spotlighted while the shoots were still tender and green. The main point is that a wide variety of experiments is necessary before a few of them may mature into models, and that any speaker or writer should avoid laying down a new law or set of regulations by which the Church is presumably to be saved.

Nevertheless, if a discussion is to be practical as well as inspiring, some guidelines must be risked. For one thing, since the false paths can be identified with considerable precision, many treatments of the crisis seem excessively negative when they avoid recommending specific cures. For another, a theology of Incarnation compels the making of concrete recommendations. If we were theologians discussing only the "heavenly flesh" of the Risen Lord, abstraction would be a temptation. But a spirit without a body is a ghost, and a discussion of renewal without specifics would be frivolous. Fortunately, there is a growing body of literature in the field, and the experiences of one "laboratory" can be checked against those of others.

For the purposes of our discussion, two situations will be reported which should help to indicate the kind of development the writer has in mind. In both cases, the attempt will be made to deal generally enough to protect the sensibilities of those involved, and graphically enough to encourage others to go and do likewise.

One experiment is current: *The Chicago Ecumenical Institute.* The Institute is ecumenical, being a department of the Church Federation of Greater Chicago. It is based on an Order, with a strong discipline governing the common life. The other example is now history: *Mount Olivet Community Church in Dearborn, Michigan,* during the decade beginning in the summer of 1936. These years cover the war years in one of our major industrial concentrations. They also cover the years of extreme tension during which the dominant company in the area passed from feudalism to enlightened participation in community and national affairs. The congregational life in this period was one of remarkable spiritual health and Christian discipline. Both examples of Christian life—the Chicago Ecumenical Institute and Mount Olivet Community Church—are worthy of study, for their achieve-

ment in quality of Christian commitment and their participation in the life of the society at large.

THE CHICAGO ECUMENICAL INSTITUTE

The Institute as presently constituted is a merger of two
histories. In 1954, following the Evanston meeting of the
Assembly of the World Council of Churches, an Institute
was set up in Evanston to carry on in North America the
kinds of programs offered in Europe by the Ecumenical Institute at Bossey, near Geneva, Switzerland. This consisted
chiefly of study seminars and conferences, conducted on an
open and interdenominational basis, directed to the main
problems confronting the Christian churches in mid-twentieth
century. In 1960 this program and some property were taken
over by a team which moved from the Austin (Texas) Faith-
in-Life Community. The new community, which also com-
prised the staff of the Institute, greatly enlarged the educational program and set out to develop models of "imaginal
learning." That is, the problems of Chicago's west side—90
per cent Negro, laced with unemployment and tormented by
slum conditions—were given attention and the new style of
education was integrated into the common life of the Order
and its program of disciplined life and service. The new style
of work has been described as follows:

The Ecumenical Institute . . . understands itself to be vitally related
to the three over-arching emphases that have characterized the church
in recent years; a theological resurgence in which the Church has been
engaged in re-thinking its comprehensive self-understanding and mission, the lay movement involving many experiments among the laity
to embody their recovered mission in and to the world, and the movement of ecumenicity oriented in a fresh sense toward the mission of the
Church at the most localized level.[8]

One of the liveliest centers of new thought and experiment in Christendom, the Chicago Ecumenical Institute is carried by an Order with a discipline. At this level, it is one of the "evangelical communities"—a type of renewal movement previously discussed. The Board of the Institute, like the Church Federation of Greater Chicago to which the program is organically related, functions primarily as a channel to interpret the work to society at large. Board members also help to relate the Institute to other centers of concern through such means as the "Chicago Hot-line" (founded in January, 1966)—a weekly telephone conference which hooks together fourteen points and some 275 participants. The Order, however, underwrites the entire work with shared income, shared spiritual discipline, and shared "Moral Covenant and Corporate Discipline."

The Order has three categories of members. In 1967 there were ten Permanent Members, five Fellows of the Order, and a number of Interns or Novices (resident on a one-year basis). The members of the Order live together at the Institute, in buildings purchased from the Bethany Theological Seminary in 1964. Each family is allotted dormitory-type rooms, the number depending upon the size of the family. There are common meals throughout the week, with the exception of Thursday, when each family has the afternoon and evening in private. Pooling their income, the Order sets aside money to provide for occasional travel and for the education of their children.

The style of association calls for government by what the Quakers have long called "the sense of the meeting" rather than by vote-taking.

No issue is submitted to vote, but instead, after sufficient discussion, decision is arrived at by consensus. The mechanics are as follows: At any time that there seems to be some agreement—over any question that is being discussed, anyone may state the matter as the consensus of the group. It will then be so unless someone disagrees or states un-readiness to arrive at that consensus without further discussion. The procedure assures unity and speed of decision in a way that strict ad-herence to Parliamentary Procedure cannot. Every member is fully bound to the procedure arrived at by consensus, and so every member eagerly participates in the discussion that leads to that consensus.[9]

This manner of government, which has spread from the Order itself to associated cadres in local churches, is—if prop-erly operative—sensitive and apostolic beyond anything reached by counting votes. At the same time—and this leads to criticism by "out-groupers"—if the more experienced and aggressive members are not careful of the sensibilities of others it may on occasion create a new tyranny of the spirit.

Hannah Arendt warned, in a significant study of totali-tarianism, of the dangers which emerge when the elite group, surrounded by sympathizers, gives insufficient attention to the opinions of those "outside."

The members of the elite group are wholly identified with the move-ment: they have no profession and no private life independent from it. The sympathizers constitute a protective wall around the members of the movement and represent the outside world to them.[10]

All new movements of vigor and discipline in the Church run this danger, and the more they lean upon the secret disci-pline of the apostolic type, the more they invent their own language and recognition signs ("ecstatic utterance"), the more danger they run. The only corrective force, lest the movement in time flatten out into its own esoteric and im-pacted style of culture-religion, is to remain genuinely "open to the world." This the Institute purposes to do by a program of vigorous Christian action on Chicago's west side—the "Fifth City," as they call it.

The Institute staff is convinced that the ghetto Negro is victimized primarily by a self-image which is self-defeating: he feels that he cannot make choices, cannot act, cannot shape his destiny. Controlled by the relentless fates, he sees himself doomed to defeat, with only occasional release in spontaneous outcry or violence. The Institute has therefore undertaken to develop a model "Fifth City" in the overwhelmingly Negro area surrounding the center. At present about one hundred Negroes are enlisted as "Iron Men," leading the stakes and guilds into which sympathizers have been divided. Although the problem of remolding a whole society is large, it should be noted that during summer racial violence on Chicago's west side in 1967 no incidents occurred in the Fifth City. While fear was rampant in many other areas, the young adults of the Fifth City were able to go ahead on one of the worst days of the "long, hot summer" with a friendly street dance. By spring, 1968, the fuse had burned shorter and the Institute itself experienced a flurry of conflict with black gangs.

The Institute is committed to the renovation of the local congregation, and in this respect it contrasts sharply with some "renewal" movements which have written off the institutional church as a bad job. The style of work is based on the disciplined Christian "cell" or "cadre" (in Acts, "house church"; in Wesleyan history, the "class meeting"; in home missions of early nineteenth-century America, the "band") working within the congregation. Such a group defines itself as a cadre of local church members who have decided to be the Church, and to channel the energy and resources of the congregation into the history-making process. Again, the theology of action and the insistence upon personal decision tend to "bring not peace, but a sword."

Some resent being required to decide; others find it emancipating and life-giving. The psychology of the initiates is that of those who are "free in bondage"—if Christ is central, a distinctly Pauline type of religious experience. Since so many congregations are anything but "a community of faithful people," the politics of the cadres tends to be resented by those whose self-image involves identity with existing institutions and structures. To be specific, some church leaders, critical of the "authoritarian discipline" of the cadres, have forbidden pastors and congregations under their supervision to give Institute representatives a hearing. Although uttered in defense of freedom, such commands are of course simply the resistance of old institutions to new structure-forming energies. "Freedom" in this sense nowhere exists, and if it did it would still have little to do with the yoke of Christ. Among those who take the dialogue earnestly, and believe experiment to be necessary, the members of the Order are accorded a hearing.

The outreach of the Institute goes far beyond the Fifth City, however. The Institute carries on, in fact, a major educational program. In 1964, 450 students attended courses; in 1965, 8,000; in 1966, over 17,000. The forty-four-hour weekend study sessions, which afford a basic orientation in "thinking Christianly," are a kind of "pressure cooker" for mind and spirit. The time is used most intensively, and some are thoroughly alienated. But those to whom it is startling and refreshing that the claims of Christ are put so demandingly, the forty-four-hour weekend is often a turning point not unlike the most dramatic of Pauline or Wesleyan conversions. Recognizing that the process of unlearning is often as basic as learning anew, the teaching staff frankly speaks of its shock approach in the initial stages as "brainwashing." Once the purifying process is under way, a radically existentialist theology based primarily on Barth, Bonhoeffer, Bultmann, the

Niebuhrs, and Tillich is presented bindingly. The student is required to answer Yes or No: he is not allowed to sit on the balcony, to enjoy the dialogue and merely consider it "interesting."

The approach is strongly reminiscent of evangelical and pietist views of the importance of personal decision and commitment. (As a matter of fact, Søren Kierkegaard—the father of the modern existentialist line of attack on culture-religion—was deeply and directly influenced by the Moravians.) But, all genetic questions aside, it is hard to deny that in a period of history where most of the baptized regard Christianity as one of the useful social forces, any real good must come from centers marked above all by moral earnestness. The trouble with much that passes for "education" in our churches as well as outside is that although it sometimes leads to verbal orthodoxy it rarely leads to orthodoxy of life. What is lacking in most congregations today is the quality of moral earnestness. It is common in some scurrilous circles to criticize the churches or councils of churches because their theology is not sound. This can be debated but hardly resolved with clarity in a time of changing words and changing structures. A "theology of Christian atheism" put forward by a just man is certainly more pleasing to the God of the Bible than the Apostles' Creed mouthed by a wicked racist. But verbal orthodoxy is not the issue: the issue is a thoroughgoing concern to "do the truth." By this test, the Ecumenical Institute rates very high on the map of world Christianity.

MOUNT OLIVET COMMUNITY CHURCH

In the summer of 1936 a new pastor came to the pulpit of this congregation. He was a nationally known leader of young people's work in the Methodist Episcopal Church, a specialist in small-group work and the methods of spiritual life retreats, and an officer in several Christian social action movements. The new pastor's wife was prominent in women's work in the church and in missionary societies.

As early as 1934 the new pastor had written a major article on the use of fellowship groups in training the church laity, and he participated later in the annual sessions of the Conference on Disciplined Life and Service (1939–49). The Christian education work of the congregation was undergirded, by steady persuasion and instruction, by a careful foundation in weekly face-to-face fellowship in small covenant groups. Those who joined in the house churches came in response to preaching and personal invitation, but a definite effort was made to see to it that all Board members and organizational officers sooner or later be persons with a personal experience and profession of religion. The groups were thus open to develop new leaders and at the same time many of those to whom giving leadership in the local church had become a habit were able to recover the excitement of the first love of Christ.

During the period of intensive cultivation—and it takes approximately seven or eight months for a "fellowship group" to gain its strength and begin to form new men and new women—little could be done of the usual popular evangelism. For two years, reports of statistical gains made to the annual conference were unimpressive. If time is spent in laying careful foundations, it is simply not available for door-to-door calling to pick up unattached individuals. But the foundation was laid, and laid well, and by the time of testing there were over sixty persons in key positions in the congregation who had spent many months in weekly meeting to equip themselves as better Christians. They had studied the Bible together, prayed together, gone on retreats together, talked of the Christian attitude to race, peace, missions, social justice.

The time of testing came with the final drive of the United Automobile Workers to organize the Ford Motor Company. Today, thirty years later, it is very difficult even for those who lived through it to remember the violence and terror which dominated labor relations before the Wagner Act. Five years later the Ford Motor Company, under the old Henry—isolationist, anti-Semite, sponsor of British-Israelite radio broadcasts, and mechanical genius—was still defying the law of the land on labor's right to organize. The company's stand against collective bargaining, maintained in announced defiance of the President, the Supreme Court, and the Congress, was enforced by a private army of thugs commanded by Harry Bennett. Bennett, boasting that he would "never recognize the UAW 'til hell froze over," set out to break the union by beatings, firings, and black-listing.

When the courts finally compelled an election for the collective bargaining agent, the company attempted to hedge its bets by sponsoring another "union"—ostensibly AFofL. Head of the alternative "union" was Homer Martin, once a Baptist preacher, then a union organizer, and finally a renegade from both church and labor. The voting laborers were thus offered three choices: (1) UAW (CIO), (2) Martin's AFofL "union," (3) no union at all.

On the evening before the UAW (CIO) organizing drive was launched, the UAW asked the pastor of Mount Olivet to issue a public statement on the issues at stake. He had for years followed the requirement of *The Discipline* of the Church, to read from the pulpit "The Social Creed of the Church" once a year. In the creed the right of labor to organize and bargain collectively is affirmed. He was offered freedom to say whatever he wanted to say, with the assurance that the UAW newspaper would print it in full the next day. This was his Gethsemane.

What shall a conscientious Christian pastor do in such circumstances? If he is a "kept" man, a false prophet in the scriptural sense of the word, he will make his peace with the company (indeed, he would have done it long before) —identifying company violence and illegality with "law and order." There are literally dozens of Protestant churches in the Deep South today where the battles of the past are still being fought, where the ministers receive monthly company checks under the table—and keep still. If he is a decent fellow, but timorous, he will keep still on important issues affecting his people and confine his efforts to the individual and family-centered religion. If he is a man of some public concern, but no lover of conflict, he will take the traditional path: to urge all citizens to vote, but avoid specifics. What, however, if he is true to his calling to preach the truth and to serve Him who is Lord of all life?

On the opening day of the drive the UAW newspaper carried the pastor's picture and his counsel: "Vote CIO!" He stated what Christianity taught in the matter of social justice, condemned what the company had done in violation of the Law of the Bible and the law of the land, exposed the fraudulent purpose of the company union, and counseled the working men to vote to end this bondage. This they did, in overwhelming numbers.

The company recognized the union. A few months later, Henry Ford II took the reins of management and dismissed Bennett and his private army. He hired John S. Bugas, until then head of the FBI office in Detroit and a man of outstanding character and probity, to take charge of personnel and security. Within a short time, and ever since, Ford has been noted for its industrial peace, its enlightened treatment of persons, and its constructive role in the life of the nation.

From the viewpoint of responsible Christianity, the effect of the experience on the congregation, many of whom were in the office and management of Ford or on the assembly line, was noteworthy. Out of nearly six hundred members, two resigned: they simply could not stand it to see their minister taking a public position against the company. The rest held fast in Christian fellowship and discipline. There were of course a number who disagreed with the pastor's viewpoint, but they understood the importance of the liberty of preaching and a free pulpit. They valued what they shared in Christ more than popular opinion or prejudice. They had passed through the water together and so they were able to pass through the fire together.

It would be cheapening to stress the subsequent successes of the congregation, which were many. But those who peddle cheap grace and justify slovenly membership standards by statistical success have created the impression that careful attention to teaching and discipline will cost the church participants and support. Sometimes this may be so, but in this case it was not. At the end of the period of setting standards and training members thoroughly, after the time of testing, the congregation grew rapidly in numbers and in giving to benevolences. The reason is plain: sixty-five ministers are more effective than one or two, in evangelism as well as social witness. By taking the pains to ensure a sound and well-trained core of disciplined Christians, the pastor in effect built a group ministry, one that was capable of joy and faithfulness in adversity as well as in good times.

All active church people are familiar with the notion that

the preacher's job is to be "right" on issues. There are even churches where lay people will tolerate the preacher's taking positions they believe to be contrary to "common sense" and threatening to the church's "good reputation." The minister's true and pastoral function, however, is to raise up a people capable of being the Church in fair weather and foul. Under pressure as difficult as a congregation could encounter, the fellowship of Mount Olivet maintained the church's ministry: with the same Lord, and a common style of life, they overcame the social pressures and temptations and represented together in one place the Universal Church.

The primary fault where the church fails to be the Church is not lack of values or lack of principles: it is lack of formation, lack of discipline, lack of the sacramental bond which the Spirit can and does give to those who truly practice His presence. Today, with the spiritual underworld as strong as it is in America, with many churches caught up in the preliminary stage of a church struggle just as real as that in the German Third Reich or in Communist societies, the minister who fails to preach and maintain membership training and membership standards is no true pastor at all. He is, as John Wesley once said of peddlers of cheap grace who neglect to train the laity in frequent use of the means of grace, "but raising children for the Murderer."

The conclusion is plain to all who have ears to hear and eyes to see: The time has come to cut through the comfortable culture-religion into which so many of our churches have settled, to become more disciplined in the life which is in Christ, and to become more openhearted and generous in the life of the world's work and the public forum.

▶ NOTES

1 WHY ARE WE CONFUSED?

1. Walter Prescott Webb, *The Great Frontier* (Boston: Houghton Mifflin Co., 1952).
2. Robert E. Speer, *The Church and Missions* (New York: George H. Doran Co., 1926), pp. 121–22.
3. Eliezer Berkovits, "Judaism in the Post-Christian Era," XV *Judaism* (1966), 1:74.
4. Rolf Hochhuth, *The Deputy* (New York: Grove Press, 1964), p. 226.
5. André Schwarz-Bart, *The Last of the Just* (New York: Bantam Books, 1962), p. 412.
6. *Methodist News* (Los Angeles), November 4, 1965 release.
7. *The New York Times* (November 5, 1965), p. 38 n.
8. *Time* magazine, vol. 86, no. 17, pp. 61–62.

2 THE THREE PERIODS OF AMERICAN CHURCH HISTORY

1. Quotation in Fred Clarke, *et al.*, *Church, Community, and State in Relation to Education* (London: Allen & Unwin, 1938), p. 71.
2. Timothy L. Smith, *Revivalism and Social Reform* (Nashville: Abingdon Press, 1957), p. 12 *et passim.*
3. Joseph Story, *Commentaries on the Constitution* (Boston: Little, Brown & Co., 1891), 5th edition, par. 1873. First published in 1838.
4. Benjamin Lyon Smith, *Alexander Campbell* (St. Louis: Bethany Press, 1930), pp. 259–60.
5. Daniel Dorchester, *Christianity in the United States* (New York: Hunt & Eaton, 1895), revised edition, p. 350.
6. Franklin H. Littell, *The Free Church* (Boston: Beacon Press, 1957), p. 117.

7. The March 1957 Current Population Survey (CPS) of the U.S. Bureau of Census: "Religion Reported by the Civilian Population of the United States: March, 1957," *Current Population Reports,* No. 79 (February 2, 1958), p. 20.

8. James Baldwin, "Letter from a Region in My Mind," *The New Yorker* (November 17, 1962), pp. 59 ff., 142.

9. Martin E. Marty, *The New Shape of American Religion* (New York: Harper & Row, 1958), p. 28.

10. C. C. Goen, *Revivalism and Separatism in New England, 1740–1800* (New Haven: Yale University Press, 1962).

11. Edwin Scott Gaustad, *Historical Atlas of Religion in America* (New York: Harper & Row, 1962), pp. 158 ff.

12. Quoted in Ronald E. Osborn, *The Spirit of American Christianity* (New York: Harper & Row, 1958), p. 31.

13. Menno Simons, *The Complete Writings of Menno Simons* (Scottsdale, Pa.: Herald Press, 1956), in "Exhortation to the Magistrates," p. 202.

14. *Ibid.,* in "Reply to Gellius Faber," p. 779.

15. Helmut Gollwitzer, "True Freedom," in Franklin H. Littell (ed.), *Sermons to Intellectuals* (New York: Macmillan Co., 1963), p. 84.

16. Quoted in David H. Schaff, *The Life of Philip Schaff* (New York: Charles Scribner's Sons, 1897), p. 472.

3 THE FUTURE OF THE AMERICAN WORLD CITY

1. In their important studies, Will Herberg (*Protestant–Catholic–Jew*) and Gerhard Lenski (*The Religious Factor*) have shown that it is imperative to distinguish the power of the faith communities from the function of churches and synagogues, as such.

2. John XXIII, *Pacem in Terris* (April 10, 1963); in the *New York Times,* CXII (April 11, 1963), sec. C, pp. 17–19.

3. Cf. Mathew Ahmann (ed.), *Race: Challenge to Religion* (Chicago: Henry Regnery Co., 1963).

4. From material prepared by the coordinating staff of Chicago Dialog: "Chicago Dialog Prospectus, Participation Form" (March, 1967), quoted from *Look* magazine (March 21, 1967), p. 18.

5. Marshall McLuhan, *Understanding Media: The Extensions of Man* (New York: McGraw-Hill, 1964), p. 4.

4 THE AGE OF DIALOGUE

1. Murray A. Gordon, "The Unconstitutionality of Public Aid to Parochial Schools," in Dallin H. Oaks (ed.), *The Wall between Church and State* (Chicago: University of Chicago Press, 1963), p. 94.
2. *The New York Times* (March 28, 1964), p. 21.
3. J. M. Shea, Jr., "Memo from a Dallas Citizen," XXVIII *Look* (1964), 6:88 f. Mr. Shea was subsequently dismissed by Petrofino, Inc.
4. Hendrik Kraemer, "Over de moglijkheid van dialoog met de 'ongelovige'," XIII *Wending* (1959), 11:724–66.
5. Cf. Ernst Benz, *Kirchengeschichte in Ökumenischer Sicht* (Leiden & Köln: E. J. Brill, 1961), Chapter V.
6. In A. F. Carrillo de Albornoz, *The Basis of Religious Liberty* (New York: Association Press, 1963), p. 161.
7. Cf. Kurt Hutten and Siegfried von Kortzfleisch (eds.), *Asien missioniert im Abendland* (Stuttgart: Kreuz-Verlag, 1962).

5 THE NEW STYLE OF CORPORATE LIFE

1. Charles R. Adrian, *Governing Urban America* (New York: McGraw-Hill, 1955), pp. 16–17.
2. Edwin Scott Gaustad, *Historical Atlas of Religion in America* (New York: Harper & Row, 1962), pp. 43–44, 160–61.
3. *Select Letters* (New York: G. P. Putnam's Sons, 1933), p. 39.
4. John Osman, "A City Is a Civilization," in Robert Lee (ed.), *Cities and Churches: Readings on the Urban Church* (Philadelphia: Westminster Press, 1962), p. 75.
5. Peter L. Berger, "Community in Modern Urban Society," in *Cities and Churches, op cit.*, p. 69.
6. Truman A. Douglass, "The Job the Protestants Shirk," in *Cities and Churches, op. cit.*, p. 88.
7. Eugen Gerstenmeier, "Diakonat," in Franklin H. Littell and Hans Hermann Walz (eds.), *Weltkirchenlexikon: Ein Handbuch der Oekumene* (Stuttgart: Kreuz-Verlag, 1960), col. 274.
8. Translated by Franklin H. Littell, *The German Phoenix* (New York: Doubleday & Co., 1960), Appendix B; see also Arthur C.

Cochrane, *The Church's Confession under Hitler* (Philadelphia: Westminster Press, 1962), *passim*.

9. Paul Gürtler, *Nationalsozialismus und evangelische Kirchen im Warthegau* (Göttingen: Vandenhoeck und Ruprecht, 1958), Appendix, Document 8.

10. "Die Kirchen in der Deutschen Demokratischen Republik," in Joachim Beckmann (ed.), *Kirchliches Jahrbuch: 1958* (Gütersloh: Gütersloher Verlagshaus Gerd Mohn, 1959), p. 199.

11. William J. Villaume (ed.), *Policy and Strategy in Social Welfare . . . Report to the Churches* (New York: National Council of Churches, 1957), pp. 29–30

12. Dietrich Bonhoeffer, *Prisoner for God: Letters and Papers from Prison* (New York: Macmillan Co., 1957), p. 140.

13. Cf. George W. Webber, *God's Colony in Man's World* (Nashville: Abingdon Press, 1960).

14. Cf. Marvin T. Judy, *The Larger Parish and Group Ministry* (Nashville: Abingdon Press, 1959).

15. Cf. Littell, "Can America Adopt the Evangelical Academy?" in XLIII, *The Christian Scholar* (1960), 1:39–45.

16. Karl Barth, *Church Dogmatics, Vol. I, Part II: The Doctrine of the Word of God* (Edinburgh: T & T Clark, 1936), p. 464.

17. Dietrich Bonhoeffer, *The Cost of Discipleship* (London: SCM Press, 1948), p. 25.

18. Cochrane, *The Church's Confession under Hitler* (Philadelphia: Westminster Press, 1962).

19. "The Undivided Church in a Divided City," XXI, *Christianity and Crisis* (1961), 16:167–68.

20. Cf. Lee E. Dirks, *Religion in Action* (Silver Spring, Md.: Newsbook, 1965), pp. 176–83; Loren E. Halvorson, *Exodus into the World* (Minneapolis: Augsburg Publishing House, 1966).

21. See *The German Phoenix*, Chapter I and Appendix B.

22. Richard W. Solberg, *God and Caesar in East Germany* (New York: Macmillan Co., 1961).

6 THE SECULAR CITY AND CHRISTIAN SELF-RESTRAINT

1. Position paper, "The Christian Basis and Opportunity of the YMCA Today"; reprint from the *Record* (National Council of the YMCA's of the USA, May 13–15, 1966).

2. Langdon Gilkey, *How the Church Can Minister to the World without Losing Itself* (New York: Harper & Row, 1964), p. 136.
3. Cf. Franklin H. Littell, "Protestant Seminary Education in America," in James Michael Lee and Louis J. Putz (eds.), *Seminary Education in a Time of Change* (Notre Dame, Ind.: Fides Publishers, 1965), pp. 533–56.
4. Harvey Cox, *The Secular City* (New York: Macmillan Co., 1965; paperback).

7   THE RECOVERY OF CHRISTIAN INTEGRITY

1. Franklin H. Littell, "The Methodists," in Kyle Haselden and Martin E. Marty (eds.), *What's Ahead for the Churches?* (New York: Sheed & Ward, 1964), pp. 74–93.
2. Findley B. Edge, *A Quest for Vitality in Religion* (Nashville: Broadman Press, 1963), pp. 204 f.
3. Duncan Howlett, *The Fourth American Religion* (New York: Harper & Row, 1964); cf. my review in *The Chicago Theological Seminary Register*, LV (1965), 8:41–42.
4. Franklin H. Littell, "Some Free Church Remarks on the Concept, The Body of Christ," in Robert S. Pelton (ed.), *The Church as the Body of Christ* (Notre Dame, Ind.: University of Notre Dame Press, 1963), pp. 127–38.
5. *The New York Times* (March 26, 1964), p. 33.
6. Wesley Baker, *The Split-Level Fellowship* (Philadelphia: Westminster Press, 1965).
7. Philip A. Anderson, *Church Meetings That Matter* (Boston: United Church Press, 1965), pp. 11–12.
8. Donald G. Bloesch, *Centers of Christian Renewal* (Boston: United Church Press, 1964).

8   A TEACHING CHURCH

1. Dietrich Bonhoeffer, *Creation and Fall* (New York: Macmillan Co., 1959), pp. 35, 38.
2. Bonhoeffer, *Life Together* (New York: Harper & Row, 1954), p. 38.
3. *Ibid.*, p. 8.
4. *Ibid.*, p. 37.

5. J. Brooke Mosley, *Christians in the Technical and Social Revolutions of Our Time* (Cincinnati: Forward Movement Publications, 1966), pp. 33–34.

6. Otto Dibelius, *Grenzen des Staates* (Tübingen: Furche-Verlag, 1949), p. 83.

7. *Lumen Gentium* (November 21, 1964), Chapters II, VII; in Walker M. Abbott (ed.), *The Documents of Vatican II* (New York: Guild Press/America Press/Association Press, 1966).

8. *Image,* Journal of the Ecumenical Institute (January, 1963), Vol. I, No. 1, p. 1.

9. "The Local Congregation Covenant Group (Congregational Cadre) as a Nucleus of the Church in Missional Motion"; unpublished paper of the Chicago Southeast Sector Cadre (July, 1966), pp. 6–7.

10. Hannah Arendt, *The Origins of Totalitarianism* (New York: Harcourt, Brace & Co., 1951), p. 367.

▶ INDEX

▶ INDEX